Introduction

I have written these poems with a purpose. I want to share my miraculous journey from Borderline Personality Disorder, Generalized Anxiety, and Clinical Depression, to now living a life that I truly love to live.

I have read this book over and over again in the process of editing, and each time I read it, I gain greater insight into what it means to live a powerful spiritual life. Spiritual living is not religion; in fact, it probably is the farthest thing from religion. Religion involves group dynamics focussing on a higher power, whereas spiritual living is a very personal journey into our own inner self, our heart and soul.

I have made the journey from wanting to end it all to waking up each day in awe of just how magical this life really is. It is indeed an enchanted life. It is my hope that my love for life will flow from my heart into your heart through the enchantment of this collection of thoughts and poems.

1

Copy rite
Three Ravens Productions
Lawrence J.W. Cooper
ISBN: 9781688373945
Create Space and Amazon Books
August, 2018 Part 1

Enchanted with Life

My search continues, season by season, moment by moment,
Seeking solutions to questions that I can't understand,
Scanning the horizons of my world for enchantment,
Magic that will surpass the limits of time and mind.

But the answers are not in the mysticism of miracles,
Nor in the beauty that surrounds my world;
The answers lie within the minute particles
Of the substance of the energy of my inner soul.

Herein lies the essence of my being,
The higher portion of my sentient life's purpose and goal.
Herein lies the mystery of peace and contentment,
The fragments of being and thought that make me whole.

Herein is my Higher Self, complete with just a piece of me.
Herein is my mystical self that longs for connection
With all that by chance is and all that will ever be.
Herein swims my essence in the magic of the enchanted sea.

Five Steps to Grounding

Grounding is a spiritual term defining a process whereby we become rooted in our physical and emotional states. For our purposes, I have composed this simple definition:

Grounding is a spiritual function that helps us create a bridge between the physical (body), mental (mind), and spiritual (soul) parts of our being. Grounding opens up the door to self-actualization.

I have identified five qualities that will help us form a grounding for living a purposeful and joyous life. They are:

- Belief,
- Self-Awareness,
- Self-Acceptance,
- Discernment,
- Forgiveness.

We will begin with Belief.

Week 1 - Belief

The human mind has to believe in something, but we can choose what we believe, and that makes all the difference. The mind is made up of a complex system of neural bundles that connect processing centers to our prefrontal cortex that together make our mind states or beliefs. These mind states are made up of past images, memories, thoughts, and emotions. Whenever the mind is confronted with a new situation, it checks these mind states and acts according to these beliefs. Beliefs then influence our thoughts, and these thoughts produce our actions. Left to its own devices, the mind will act automatically accordingly to its own physical and mental needs, wants, and desires.

However, we have another resource which I refer to as the Higher Self that can serve as a check and balance on our mind. The Higher Self is a combination of heart and soul. The soul focuses on the greater good for our self and mankind in general, while the heart links the spiritual with the temporal through the power of love. Together they constitute the Higher Self.

I have used the upper case letters for the Higher Self to emphasize that we are more than just organic beings; we share in something beyond just our physical humanity. It is through our belief in our Higher Self that we become spiritual people, opening up a vast pool of resources through which we can become beautiful and powerful beings. It is my hope that whenever we see these upper case letters, we may realize just how beautiful and powerful we truly are.

Week 1, Day 1
I believe in my Higher Self

Due to the influences of our western world, I had become fragmented. I no longer held the belief that I was designed to live as one self, composed of body, mind, and soul. When I reintegrated these three components, I began to function as a whole being, as my Higher Self.

I have come to realize that belief, or faith, is the voice of my Higher Self. It is my voice of creative imagination. It is my voice of love. Faith allows me to see how things are and to dream how things can be. Faith tells me that I am a beautiful and powerful being with the ability to create a life that I can truly love to live.

Collectively, faith helps us to change this world in which we live into a new and better place.

I Believe

I rejoice in my power to believe.
Through the wisdom of my mind and heart,
I live to design, to create, and to fashion,
A piece of my own reality that is magical.

I create hope from the fragments of despair,
Possessing the wisdom to shape a thought
That can change this dark and dreary place
Into my own sanctuary, my own Shangri-La.

I believe I am sharing the power of creation
With all who weave the magic of believing.
We are changing the reality of this world
Simply and miraculously because we believe.

Together we can create this beautiful us,
Dazzling souls who transcend body and brain,
Where we can feel the breath of all that is,
And reshape our world because we believe.

Week 1, Day 2
I Belief in What I Do

I believe that this life is not just a random occurrence in a sea of chaos. There seems to be a pattern, a master plan, where all energy and matter survives and thrives according to universal laws. I believe that the energy that is in me, the energy of love, the energy that I create, is a part of that plan. I am here for a purpose, and that purpose is to grow and expand through the power of love.

I possess a unique set of tools to bring my beliefs into reality. My purpose is to write, to put thoughts into words, to create feelings that will resonate with my readers, helping them create their own vibrations which will lead them to expand and grow into the person they want to be.

My Life Work

Poetry,
My life work,
I scribble words on paper,
Believing that somehow, somewhere,
Beyond the neural circuits of my brain,
There is a sacred spirit that dwells quietly within,
Who uses my humble words to reveal
Some truth, some universal law,
That is hidden behind feelings,
Words, and images.

My life work,
My divine purpose,
Is to share the words I have created,
Images which harmonize with life's rhythms,
Taking me and my readers to the source of all wisdom.
I work my words until they yield the sustenance of life,
To be shared generously with those who hunger,
So we can face this barren life together
With the joy of our being,
And face death
With a smile.

Week 1, Day 3
I believe In My Life's Purpose

I recently sat down with my marketing coach and mapped out a course of action to market my latest book, *The Room*. However, what I ended up with was a marketing plan to market myself. I had a hard time with that. But really, isn't that what life is all about? My work is just an extension of who I am: my skills, talents, hopes, and dreams. I have to make a conscious effort to believe that I am important, and that the work I do is important, and then I have to give myself permission to be proud of who I am and what I do.

My Mind Map

My future, mapped out on paper,
Illusions and delusions put into words,
Only to be crossed out
And penciled in again,
Sorting out what is me,
What I should not be,
What I should be,
And what I can be,
Paring down daydreams and nightmares
Into drops of blood-based reality.

And I have come to realize
That I must never stifle my dreams;
I must stay true
To what is engrained in my soul,

My purpose,
My raison d'etre.

I must resist that desire from my tired mind,
That says I just need to relax on my front deck,
And watch the never ending procession of sunsets
Disappearing quietly into the Salish Sea.

And as that quiet moment of silent solitude
Weaves its magic, bringing order to the chaos,
It becomes a blazing orb of light to my dark world.
The vital energy bursts within;
That ball of pure white energy
Reveals a new beginning
Emerging from the shadows of the past,
Urging me to reshuffle my scattered thoughts,
Set my course to pursue my hopes and dreams,
And stand tall and face my critics,

Naked and unashamed.

Week 1, Day 4
I Believe in Romantic Love

I believe that love is the divine energy that binds me to the source of all life and being. According to the Greeks, there are six different kinds of love. My favorite is Eros, erotica, sensuous, playful, emotional, and passionate love, which I reserve for my life-mate. It is what makes my life worthwhile. It is my greatest source of pleasure and joy. If I believe in reincarnation, perhaps my love and I are like two old souls who have shared many previous lives and have come to Earth one last time to experience the sweet sensations of perfect love.

My Dearest

I believe in you, my dearest,
In the beauty of your aging body,
In the brilliance of your expanding self,
In the sweetness and power of your soul.

I believe that you and I have come to this,
The last stage of our long and glorious journey,
Two old souls tasting the wisdom of the ages,
Returning joyously to savour one last time
The perfect and everlasting ecstasy of love.
I believe that through our love for one another,
We have tested life in a hundred different ways,
And we have finally become one with each other.

Through the power of two,
We have bridged the gap
To the power of one,
One with each other,
One with all that is,
And all that will ever be,
In perfect peace,
In perfect harmony,
Forever and forever,

Amen.

Week 1, Day 5
I believe in the Love I Have for My Children

The power behind my ability to create is unconditional love. I believe that I can only manifest unconditional love by the love I have for my children. I have transferred the essence of my body, mind, and soul to them. There are no conditions. I love them just for who they are.

My Dear Children

I believe in the lives I have created,
Born from the genes of my body,
Guided by the thoughts of my mind,
Enriched by the eternal breath
From the shared essence of my soul,
And nurtured by the love of my heart
That beats for them and with them.

They have all grown and left the nest,
And taken flight like birds on the wind;
They have learned to sing their own song,
And find their own food of life,
To be shared with the bodies and souls
Of the ones they themselves have created.

And when we meet from time to time,
Our eyes still delight in a smile,
    Our bodies in a hug
    Our hearts in a kiss,
Our minds still share memories
That only we hold and cherish,
And our souls still resonate with sweet vibrations,
As we share the love,
    That is the essence of eternity,
        Now and forever.

Week 1, Day 6
I believe in my Fellow Human Beings

There is another kind of love that the Greeks referred to as agape love. This in essence is the positive feelings and vibrations I share with my fellow man. It is birthed by my Higher Self and is manifested in acts of kindness.

I Believe in We the People

I believe in we the people,
Engaged in the sacred process
Of discovering who we really are,
Seeking a holy path amidst the chaos,
Discovering our rightful place in the sun,
Offering a kind and gentle hand to each other,
Thereby reaching the magic of a mystical world,
A brilliant place to try out our wings and joyfully soar,
Basking in the knowledge of how far, how high, we can fly.

I have sunk my roots deep into the garden of conscious souls,
I am an eternal flower blossoming into everlasting beauty,
Growing in magnificence in Mother Earth's fertile fields,
In season after season of soft fresh moist winds,
Nurtured by the eternal energy of divine light,
Growing steadfastly into an eternal being,
Expanding beyond the limits
Of space and time.

I believe we the people
Are evolving and expanding,
Building the collective power of many,
A transcending body of pure divine energy
Expanding through limitless expanses of time,
Knowing we are indeed the children of the universe.

I believe there was no beginning, there will be no end.
When this life ends another life will surely begin.
As we enter the cocoon of death and rebirth,
We will emerge as divine beings of light,
And take flight as beautiful spirits,
Continuing to expand, and grow,
A never-ending journey
Into all that is.

Week 1, Day 7
I Believe in Life after Death

I recently attended a funeral for a ninety-two year old friend who had lived a full and rich life. As in so many life celebrations, thoughts turned to a hoped for afterlife. We all wished that he would fulfill his dream to rejoin the love of his life, his wife of sixty-two years.

I know that belief in a heaven and hell is based on religious mythology, but myths are just stories that reveal a hidden truth. I believe that this body is mortal, but we also have an essence that is pure energy. Since this energy can never be lost, I believe it is simply transformed into pure spirit.

I believe that death is not to be feared. There is no hell. I believe that if there is an afterlife, or another life, it will be free of pain and suffering. I believe that the power of belief is a gift from the source. It is the essence of faith and hope. It is the essence of our being. It is the shoulder we can lean on when life seems too hard to bear. It is the magic we can spin to create a life that we can truly love to live.

No Need to Fear Death

Knowing all there is to know and being all there is to be,
It is now time to celebrate the last days of the last life,
    That I will ever live.

However, there are still these last few years to savour,
The thrill of sensing all that my eyes can see,
    And hearing all my ears can hear.

As I caress the substance of all my hands can touch,
My soul transforms all these gifts of my senses
    Into feelings that expand into ecstasy.

As my soul captures the joys of this divine present,
It molds this ever expanding divine source of energy
    Into a shape I know will last forever.

Week 2
Self-Awareness

By definition, awareness is, "the quality or state of knowledge and understanding that something is happening or exists." When we apply that to spiritual living, we have knowledge that we exist spiritually based on our inner feelings and an understanding that we have another dimension beyond the physical. We have a Higher Self. Life's journey into Self-Awareness then is to understand the full dimensions of our physical and spiritual existence. When we stay focused on the duality of our human nature, we become aware that we are beings of unlimited power.

Week 2, Day 1
Being Mindful

The beginning of Self-Awareness is mindfulness. In my view, mindfulness is simply closing down the rational part of my brain and opening up my whole being to all the sensations around me. It is focusing on the beauty of this world. It can be a walk along the ocean shore with the pungent scent of the salty air. It can be a stroll through an old growth forest with light filtering down through the maples and the scent of decaying vegetation filling my nostrils. It can be the sound of my bird friends greeting the new day by singing their hearts out about the joy of living. Mindfulness is immersing my soul in the sweet energies of nature and shutting down the noise of this world and the negative energy of my negative thoughts.

The Beauty of Nothing

There is beauty in nothing,
There is no urgency in nothing,
No need to fill it up with something,
No need for an adrenalin rush,
No need to accumulate knowledge,
No need to make something happen.
There is beauty in the moment,
There is an aliveness of feeling,
Not what is within the mind,
But that which flows through the senses,
And into the soul.

There is beauty in turning sensations to feelings,
That do not have to be defined or labelled.
There is beauty in taking those feelings,
And recreating sensations
Through poetry, music, or the canvas,
Not to agonize or scrutinize,
But to just feel and allow life to flow.

There is beauty in being,
And bringing that being to life,
By opening up my heart
To the love energy
That surrounds me,
And sharing that energy
With the ones I love.

Week 2, Day 2
I Am the Presence

Above all, I have come to realize that I am **the presence** in all things of beauty. My soul is interacting with all the sweet sensations and vibrations that surround me. Once in this state of **self-awareness**, I can feel the surge of positive energy that runs through my heart and soul. I truly understand that there are no limitations on how much I can experience and contribute to the life-flow that surrounds me. I interact with nature and other human beings with an incredible exchange of energy and being.

Just Breathing

Morning breaks,
And the dawn light filters
Through my Eastern window,
And the birds begin to sing
Their cheerful morning songs,
Welcoming the new day.

And I brew my morning cup of fresh coffee,
And dedicate the next precious hour to me,
To enjoy those things that stir my soul.

Breathing, just breathing,
Feeling the air laden with oxygen
Freshly created by my friends the plants and trees,
Enriched with the musty smells of decaying vegetation,
Spiced with the saltiness of the ocean breeze.

And I breathe,
Deeply, mindfully, conscious of my diaphragm
Pressing against my lungs and then opening up again
To the next wave of air mixed with the pleasure of living,
Conscious of the delights of my breathing.

And I live;
My body tingles with excitement,
As the essence of life flows into every cell.
My mind lies blissfully, peacefully in a bed of joy,
Knowing that the cares of this world have evaporated
For a precious moment beyond the boundaries of time.

Week 2, Day 3
Living Within My Higher Self

The key to developing Self-Awareness is to trust in the synchronicity of my body, mind, and soul. If I allow my Higher Self to become fragmented by the cares of this world, my mind or ego will carry me on to a never ending litany of evaluation and judgement, and that is where the confusion and pain comes in. My body will absorb the negative energies of my mind and produce adrenalin and cortisone that interrupts the flow of love energy from my heart.

However, my mind is not who I am; it is merely the instrument my Higher Self uses to turn my dreams and thoughts into reality. My Higher Self is also the grounding force of my heart and soul; it works through my mind and body to keeps me in the real world. My Higher Self is my source of imagination and creative thought. It longs to dream, grow, and expand, feeding off of the sweet vibrations of this living world. The key is to let my Higher Self lead me into living a life of peace, purpose, and joy.

The Search for the Real Me

My search continues, season by season, moment by moment,
Seeking solutions to questions I can't understand,
Scanning the horizons of my world for enchantment,
Magic that will surpass the limits of time and mind.

But the answers are not in the magic of miracles,
Nor in the beauty that surrounds my world;
The answers lie within the minute particles,
Of the substance of the energy of my inner soul.

Herein lies the essence of my being,
The higher portion of my sentient life's purpose and goal.
Herein lies the mystery of peace and contentment,
The fragments of being and thought that make me whole.

Herein is my Higher Self, complete with just a piece of me;
Herein is the mystical self that longs for connection
With all that by chance is and all that will ever be.
Herein swims my essence in the glories of the eternal sea.

Week 2, Day 4
The Source, the Tao, the Universe, and God

Through the sorrows and trials of life, I have become aware that my Higher Self is connected through my life force with the center of life itself. I believe that this presence manifests itself through a source of energy that I know as agape or unconditional love. I believe this universal love is my source of spiritual energy which flows through my heart and soul and then out into the world around me.

I need to become more aware of how my Higher Self connects with the Universal Source in order to go beyond the trials and tribulations of this mind-based life, which my mind has created, and in which it wants me to live. When I become aware of my Higher Self interacting with this Higher Power, I see only beauty and feel only love, first for myself and then for everyone and everything around me.

My Higher Power

Another day, another new day,
With all the new possibilities,
Packed full with moments of being alive.

The miracle of my human heart
Creates and gives substance
To whatever thought my mind can imagine.

And the miracle of my human soul awakens,
Seeing beyond the limits of my eyes,
And the perceptions of my brain.

Suddenly I am aware of another presence,
Which flows from the trees and other living things,
Until it envelops and excites my soul.

And gradually I become aware
Of who I really am, and why I am here,
Seeking to become the person I was meant to be.

I shall not waste this day.
I will be the most I can be,
And I will feel the most I can feel.

Then I will be more and still more,
Until this life can no longer hold
The beautiful me that is in this aging body.

Week 2, Day 5
Making the Most of Each Moment

The key to self-awareness is truly living each and every moment in my Higher Self. The essence of eternity is in this moment, which is in the now, but lasts forever. This moment in which I live while here on Earth, this life, is precious; it is my opportunity to experience the sensations of my body under the influence of my Higher Self. I stay focused on those things that are really important, those things that make my soul come alive.

This Moment

This moment in which I live,
An ever moving time capsule,
Touching the years delicately
So they will not waken,
So the dream can keep playing
Over and over again,
While I sleep away the years.

Where have they gone?
All the friends and foes?
The years filled
With the joy and pain of living?
So many years passed,
So few years yet to live.

There is an urgency now
That never was before,
To live each day to the fullest,
To experience all the mysteries,
To unwrap the unexpected
That lies in colored paper
Beneath the tree of life,
To know and understand
What it means to live,
To create a brilliant ball of energy,
That will last beyond this moment,
And blast down the door to eternity.

Week 2, Day 6
Enjoying Each and Every Day

Being aware of being truly alive is dedicating each day to growing and expanding my power to love. The key is to spend each day as though it were my last. Every morning here on Vancouver Island, I wake up to moments of glory with soft violets and pinks followed by splashes of red and gold reflecting off the Salish Sea. I walk onto my front deck, my eyes open in wonder, and I spend fifteen minutes in meditation, absorbing and enjoying just how good life is. What a way to start the day! What a way to live!

And I Would Do It All Again

Fatigue has set into my mind and body,
Threatening to destroy another day;
My heart mourns what might have been,
The loss of laughter, the time to play.

It is time to dance with the eternal beat,
Time to set aside the next thing to be done;
Time to admit my mind's defeat,
Time to bask in the glow of the evening sun.

There is no plane I need to catch;
There is no place I am compelled to go;
There is no new dream that I must hatch;
There is just this one fact I need to know:

The days fly by;
The moments roll on;
Mine is not to ask why;
Mine is to enjoy this day
Before it's gone.

The great bald eagle still graciously flies
From the tallest tree towards the sea;
The crows still chase the mighty king across the skies,
The ravens still sing their songs of comic absurdity.

And the hummer still hovers and beckons,
As it sits in the air just inches from my face;
Then as though done with its urgent inspection,
Disappears from my world without a trace.

Then that forgotten smile begins behind my eyes,
Erasing all the time—worm lines from my tired face.
Time takes one last breath before it lingers and dies,
And my spirit laughs as it resumes its rightful place.

And I pause to remember:

That the days float by;
The moments roll on;
Mine is not to ask why;
Mine is to enjoy this day
Before it's gone.

Week 2, Day 7
Life is Sacred

Life is sacred. Being truly alive is being able to look back at the past years and know I have not wasted my time on games that people play. It is being able to pass through the decades with no regrets, no sorrow for missing what might have been. My life's purpose is to erase all the negative energies that have accumulated over the years, until all that remains is positive energy, which of course is love. Being alive is to let my heart seek and create the divine energy of love which transcends time and will eventually propel me through this life and into eternity.

I Will Rise Again

The snow melts; spring waters begin their journey to the sea;
The buds on the trees awaken in the warm spring sunshine,
And the birds in pairs build their nests in the new leaves,
As nature shucks off the drab covering of winter,
And life awakens and rises again.

Bold young men pursue shy young women with words of love,
And young women lead young men on with sweet whispers;
The miracle of life echoes the sound of new born babes,
As mankind learns once again the meaning of love,
And life awakens and rises again.

People go to churches, children search for chocolate bunnies,
The ancient rites of moon and sun blend in blissful harmony,
And human kind again ponders the meaning of life and death,
As the Christ once again lays aside his flesh and blood,
And in pure spirit rises again.

I too, pass away the years in bliss, ignoring the pains of age;
I boldly stride once more into my green and golden world;
I embrace the newness of life with the wisdom of age,
And with tears of joy I embrace this new day,
And in pure spirit, I rise again.

Week 3
Discernment

By definition, discernment is, "the quality of being able to perceive, grasp, and comprehend what is obscure". On the mental and physical level, it is being able to see the intricacies and nuances of a complex situation and make an appropriate decision. When we add the spiritual dimension, we begin to see the spiritual as well as the rational aspects and consequences of the situation. It is the role of the Higher Self to view all the information and then guide the mind into the right decision for the greater good.

Week 3, Day 1
Voices

In this life, I will always hear three voices. The loudest voice is that of my ego which is constantly looking for opportunities to excel while watching for danger to my mind and body. It will always error on the side of caution, steering me away from the path of perceived danger or self-destruction. The second voice is the voice of my soul, beckoning me to live, expand, and grow by risking my level of comfort in order to contribute to the greater good. The third voice is the voice of my heart which asks me to sacrifice my sense of self for the sake of love. It is the role of my Higher Self to listen to all three voices and then make a decision for my Self within the bigger picture of life, love, and the greater good.

Dueling Voices

Voices;
So many voices,
Angry voices, laughing voices.

Voices,
Always voices,
An occasional whisper filtering through the fog,
Apologizing, filled with shame and remorse.

Voices,
Always voices,
I strain to hear the syllables of unspoken words
Being drowned out by the angry and the bold.

Stop the voices.
I can; I will;
I have the power to stop them all.

Peace, for a while,
Letting me breathe,
Letting me melt the turmoil.

And I hear the sound of laughter and love again,
Flooding my tired soul with the energy of the infinite,
Urging me to open up my heart and feel the passion,
And boldly seek the joy of each and every moment.

This voice calls me to seek the answers to questions
That I can feel inside but cannot put into words.
I need to feel them, to believe them, to trust them
To lead me to the mystical answers I seek to find.

And I am guided by a feeling, just a feeling, a vibration,
Beyond hearing and vision, beyond all my senses,
Telling me that it is okay to keep seeking for sustenance
That will allow me grow into the person I want to be.

Week 3, Day 2
The Voice of My Ego-Mind

The first step in discernment is to recognize the voice and intent of my mind. My physical mind is centered in the orbitofrontal cortex, a bundle of neurons located just behind my eyes. It has a right and left side. The left side is my rational self, my processor, or administrator. The right side is my sense of self in time and space. Along with my memories which are stored as mind states, and my processing and emotional centers, they make up what I know as my mind. It is my biological self. Its purpose is to gain knowledge so that I can better navigate through life, avoid failure and pain, and seek security, acceptance, success, and pleasure.

My mind cannot stand silence. It needs to be in control, so it will continually attempt to interrupt the silence with images and thoughts of what needs to be done for me to survive and thrive in this physical world.

Discernment

Dawn breaks.
The Eastern light brings peace
With the soft touch of wonder.
As the sensation intensifies,
I can see the fine lines of life
Held together by sweet silver threads,
That surround me,
Enfolding me in a web of joy.
My mind tries to break through
With thoughts of what must be done,

>My "to do" list,
>An objective for the day,
>A plan to plan,
>A goal to reach.

And I sit back and laugh,
At first gently,
Then from the depths of my being,
At all the confusion and pain
Manufactured by my tired mind.
And I laugh at the lack of knowing,
Because the search for knowledge,
Only leads to more questions,
While I can sit here with a smile on my face,
Because I know I have all the answers.

Week 3, Day 3
The Voice of My Soul

Discernment is being able to discern between the voice of my mind and the voice of my soul. In order to hear my soul's voice, I have to set aside the cares of the day, shut down the voice of my mind, and enter into a state of meditation. Once I enter this state of relaxation, I can prolong the silence and wait patiently for the voice of my soul. My soul's quiet voice always brings feelings of peace, love, and joy.

My Soul Voice

I have a soul; I know it; I can feel it.
Its silent energy floods my mind and body
      With sweet soft sensations,
Taking me from the mundane and the chaotic,
To the land where good dreams always come true,
      Because I create them,
Through the power of my soul-filled mind.

As I pursue the rabbits and squirrels
Through the forest that grows and flows
Past my door and into the sacred places,
I can feel the flowers sing their song of spring,
I can sense the joy of the bonded pair of eagles
That soar on the rising lifts of the warm Earth,
And my soul carries my body past the clouds
And into the clear blue skies,
That stretch from now into eternity.

Week 3, Day 4
The Voice of My Heart

If I train my mind to be still and listen, and set my heart free to feel and respond, I can hear the sounds of love that are all around me. They come to me in the form of life energy. It is the sound of the joy of just being alive, no thoughts and no worries. The voice of my heart reminds me to just let go and live life to the fullest and take time to love every minute of it.

My Heart Voice

Welcome back old friend;
It has been too long
Since I have heard your voice,
The voice of peace and contentment,
The voice that sighs,
As a sunrise spills new blood
Across a dark November sky;
The voice that moans in gratitude
To see Baynes Sound come alive again
          Out of the dark,
          And take shape
In shades of gray and blue.

It is a quiet voice,
Free of the tension
Of yelling at the cosmos,
Free of the desperate need
To be heard amidst the chaos;
It is the voice of my own heart,
Content to be just a soft whisper,
          That says it's okay
             Just to be me.

Week 3, Day 5
The Voice of My Higher Self

The voice of my Higher Self is intuition, wisdom, and the acceptance of universal truths. I recently read a good book, one I highly recommend, called The Tao of Psychology. Some of it is based on Carl Jung and the belief that true healing happens through creative imagination which occurs at the heart and soul level. The book inspired the following poem. It is about listening to the voice within that lives, breathes, and sees the true meaning of life.

Saying Good-bye to 69

Years,
I have digested them,
The bitter taste of somethings
That are meant for health and not for pleasure,
A tonic loaded with vitamins that make me healthy,
Proteins and minerals that make me strong,
And calcium what makes my backbone straighter,
But they all taste like chalk dust mixed with seaweed.

Years,
Their memories are loaded with images,
Like a play that explores the tragedies of living,
Where the hero accepts death in the final scene,
Knowing that he has conquered his greatest flaws,
And has faced life's greatest challenge.

But I am not ready to die;
I am still eager to live.
I can now move on to a string of moments
Of unending bliss and ecstasy,
Knowing what it is that is priceless,
What it is that must be held as sacred.

I am experiencing the ever-changing moment,
Filled with the opportunity
To be something beyond thought and word,
To be someone beyond the reaches of pain,
Beyond the blahness of unconsciousness.

I am a living breathing sentient being,
Conscious of what it means to be alive,
Who feels rather than understands
What it means to be a man,
What it means to love myself,
What it means to truly love my beloved wife,
What it means to love all the living moments
          That yet await me.

Week 3, Day 6
The Song of Life

The purpose of my life is to listen, feel, and enjoy the voices of every life form around me. I hear these voices through the ears of my Higher Self. These voices are felt not heard. I have to learn to listen to my feelings in order to hear the song of life. I have to quiet my mind so my heart and soul can detect and experience the sounds of harmony. They are all around me if I just take time to listen.

Voice of Life

I have discovered it from this place atop the rocks
From which I survey the works of a master,
Who carved these mountains on both sides of my island,
In majestic green topped whites amidst a sea of azure blue.

I have found it on forest paths winding around ancient trees,
In bubbling brooks harmonizing in the song of life,
In the voices of the giant eagles and the barking of sea lions
Discussing the success of the herring run.

I have found it in my country cottage sitting on my deck,
Hearing the whispering of the wind in the evergreens
As it speaks its wisdom through the giant cedars,
Beckoning me to join in the pleasures of the art of listening.

I have found it as I gaze through the skylight
At the billions of stars that shine in the night,
Free from the pollution of artificial light,
Free to shine their light into the darkness.

Above all I have found it
In the arms of a woman who tells me she loves me,
Foolishly believing that I am worthy of all her love,
Knowing that she is worthy of all the love I have to give.

Week 3, Day 7
The Voice of the Universe

I have entered the last half of the last year of my 60's. After a long battle with the voice of my mind with its nostalgia, fear, and regret, I have come to a place of peace with myself and with life. The voice of my Higher Self tells me it is okay to be 70. It is okay to just live and enjoy yet another day, and yet another year, without fear. It is okay to know that this life will eventually end because I know that another will surely begin.

Once I am in a state of harmony with life itself, I can begin to hear the silent thoughts of the universe. I can begin to understand its intricate patterns.

Patterns

There is always a brain pattern, a neural pathway,
That pursues a sequence of images and thoughts,
Leading to a plan, a set of goals, a list of objectives,
And I live and work and play according to the plan,
Passing days in constructive and destructive turmoil,
Building a life out of fragments of thought and time.

But there is another pattern, the pattern of the universe,
That is beyond the limits of my tired mind,
An underlying meaning that links all experiences,
A primal source to which I am connected,
Something that is a part of me and I am a part of it.
It exists outside of me but in me,
So that all that happens on the outside happens on the inside,
And all that happens on the inside happens on the outside.

And I am blessed by an intuitive wisdom,
That there is indeed a divine pattern linking all.
I am the eye that sees and the ear that hears,
So that I know that the natural is the supernatural,
And the supernatural is the natural;
I am separated from this pattern by thought and time,
But I am connected to all that is by the essence of ME.

Week 4
Self-Acceptance

By definition, *self-acceptance is,* "the act or state of accepting oneself, the act or state of understanding and recognizing one's own abilities and limitations". It is the opposite of self-doubt and self-judgement. When we apply this definition to conscious living, it is accepting that we are indeed spiritual beings in physical bodies. This opens up a whole new dimension where we have all the resources of the universe to accomplish whatever our mind, heart, and soul desires. We have no limitations.

However, are ability to go beyond our limitations is not based on the desires of the ego which will never be satisfied with its accomplishments. It is learning to go beyond the concepts of worldly success and focus on the expansion of our soul, our ability to create love, and pleasure of enjoying life.

Week 4, Day 1
Self-Acceptance - Awakening

Self-acceptance is more than just a group of words representing thoughts; it's a feeling. When I am truly aware of who I am, and become aware of my own powerful and eternal presence, I can sense the awakening of my soul. In turn, my Higher Self takes control of my brain and awakens every nerve cell in my body. I begin to see with the eyes of my Higher Self, and I am overpowered by my own presence. I not only accept my Self just as I am, but I am truly grateful that I have this opportunity to live a physical, spiritual, and blessed life.

Christmas Through the Ages

It comes in the middle of the sad season,
When the skies are dark and the snow falls,
In that moment where sadness covers all
With a blanket of cold.

Old days are long gone,
Hidden behind the clouds,
When life was young and free
And the sky was limitless,
And it was all okay just to be me,
Free to be all I could be.

Memories so rich,
So deeply embedded in my brain,
Sharing moments around the Christmas tree
On Christmas Eve,
Surrounded with feelings of love and belonging,
First with mother, brothers, and sisters,
Then later with wife and children,
In a warm little room with warm feelings,
When I accepted life as a gift from the gods.

And then the dark days,
When the light was distant,
And the darkness enveloped my soul,
And the next breath was hard to breathe,
And Christmas was a time for weeping,
Having lost the warmth of hugs and kisses.
Yet those days were indeed the time
When the gifts were still even more
                    Precious,
                    Priceless,
The days of enlightenment,
Paid for with tears and heartache,
When I was able to separate
The chaff from the wheat,
And dine on the bread of life.

Then as I planned another Christmas,
The day no longer held the magic of wonder;
Past moments of laughing and weeping
Were suppressed with unkind knowledge,

Cloaking the rawness of my emotions
Behind the reality of the moon and the stars,
Imprisoning my dreams of youth
With cold steel bars;
My heart was held captive to my thoughts.

But now I have become a conscious human being.
My thoughts are freed by my feelings
That say these days somehow were a blessing,
Leading me to this moment of truth,
So that I can smile and say that everything is okay;
Everything is as it should be.

And there is a new reality,
Christmas reborn,
New presents to open,
New loves to love,
New dreams to dream,
New purpose to embrace,
New gifts to give.

As I embrace the loves I have known,
That still flood my memories,
Flowing through old arteries into an old heart,
I thankfully suck in another life-giving breath,
Pumping new blood to tired tissues,
Enriching my mind with new thoughts
To be shared with a new lover,
Living in the grasp of eternity.

Week 4, Day 2
I Accept My Body Just the Way It Is

Often when I look in the mirror, I see all the blemishes and imperfections of my body. However, I acknowledge that this amazing body is still able to fulfill its purpose of feeling and experiencing. I have seven incredible senses through which I can interact with my physical world. I have these two amazing eyes that can view the wonders of nature. I have two ears to absorb the sound waves and blend them into sounds of harmony. I have millions of skin receptor cells to absorb all the sensations of the wind, the water, the sun, and above all, a loving touch from the ones I love. I have millions of receptor cells in the lining of my nose to interpret the full range of pleasant smells, from apple pie cooking in the oven, to the sweet smell of a rose. I have about fifty different receptor sells in each taste bud that can taste, recognize, and blend the very flavors of once living things. In addition, I have two powerful legs and two agile feet that can carry me to wherever the feast of my senses can best be enjoyed, and I have two arms and two hands that can hold and touch the things and the ones I love. Finally I have this wonderful brain that can integrate all these sensations and turn them into thoughts, whereby I can understand the deepest things of life. I am truly wonderfully made for the divine purpose of experiencing life to the fullest.

Forest Bath

As I stroll through these forest paths,
And stop and place my hands
On the scarred trunks
Of these centuries old forest giants,
I can feel the soft sacred vibrations,
That meet and mingle in my soul,
Slowing down the hectic pace of my mind
Into a gentle flow of sweet energy,
That lays my thoughts to rest,
So that my heart can beat out its rhythm,
And I can become a part of the harmony
Of thousands of living things.

And as I breathe in the oxygen,
And the molecules of the chemicals
Released by my dear old friends, the trees,
My body coaxes my mind
To stop and breathe slowly and deeply,
Absorbing the rich air-borne nutrients,
That flow from the tree to the air,
To my lungs, and into my bloodstream,
Enriching the very fiber of my being,
Setting each and every cell into a soft hum
That is music to my heart and soul.

Week 4, Day 3
I Accept my Stage of Life

Self-acceptance is accepting my present position in life; the seat of the elder. I have entered into my 70's, the age of wisdom. I have come to a place of peace with myself and with life, and I have discovered that it is okay to be 70. Aging does not have to be the breaking down of cells and the loss of mental function; it can be the beginning of intuitive knowledge and wisdom.

I read once that entering into eldership is the third major stage of brain development. The first is early childhood and the awakening of the cognitive mind where axons are extended and dendrites are built adding hundreds of thousands of synapses a day in the cerebral cortex. The second is adolescence where unneeded dendrites and axons are pruned and new ones are built, extending connections to new clusters of neurons, resulting in new neural pathways that represent complex thought patterns that are connected to the emotions. The third stage is entering into the wisdom of the elder. It is accompanied by growth in the corpus callosum that divides the left and right hemispheres of the brain. This is where reason and knowledge meet with insight and intuitive wisdom.

So growing older is really a special time of life where old men and old women see visions and dream dreams. It is time for us to take our place in society where we serve as elders. It is not a time to retire from contributing; it is a time to pool our resources of knowledge, wisdom and insight and bring a message of life to our lost and dying world.

I Am an Elder

I have reluctantly become the elder of my clan,
Leaving behind the body that used to scale mountains,
And the mind that designed new ways of thinking.
I have passed on my knowledge to the next generations,
Who will go on after me to places I could never go.
I have accepted my new place where I strive to be heard,
Spreading my unwanted wisdom to reluctant ears,
Who define life within the boundaries of their own minds.
I am the elder now, quietly typing away my thoughts
About what it means to live joyously and consciously;
I have surpassed the limits of my mind to go beyond time;
I have opened my heart to hear the wisdom of the universe,
Giving me tales to tell, thoughts to think, and feelings to feel.
I now believe that I am old and wise enough
To speak words that need to be heard.

I am an elder; this is a sacred time; this is holy ground.
I have taken off my shoes and walk gently on Mother Earth,
Through hallowed forest paths and on sacred ocean shores,
Feeling the consecrated life force flow through my veins.
I have tamed my tired mind and expanded my sentient soul,
So I can breathe in the wisdom and feel the fabric of life,
And translate these humble thoughts and feelings into words,
Pregnant images creating the rhythms of the universe,
So that others can be reborn and see what I see,
And feel what I feel; this is a sacred time; I am an elder.

Week 4, Day 4
I Accept My Place as a Conscious Being

Once I have accepted my Higher Self, and once I accept my station and purpose in life, and once I accept my divine place in my own world, then life becomes sweet and meaningful. I realize that I do not have to accomplish anything or be anyone other than who I am. Life circumstances and anxiety and stress cease to have any control over me. I realize my ultimate purpose is to just live, enjoy, and fill my heart to overflowing with the positive energies of joy and love. It is only through the witness of my conscious life that others may see a way through the chaos of this mind-based society in which we live.

Morning Comes Later

Morning comes later now.
The light is dimmer;
The hours seem darker.
My Hostas are no longer a brilliant green;
My Hydrangeas have lost their luster;
My Maple trees have shed
Their red and golden leaves,
Pulled in their life blood,
And stored it away from the threat
Of the icy cold winds of winter.

I am still here at five in the morning,
Contemplating life's truths,
And typing out my thoughts
So that others may seek
Their own path to transformation.
I feel the chill,
But I have added another log of warmth
To the hearth of my soul.

I am content.

Week 4, Day 5
I Accept My Limitations as a Mortal Being

I accept that my days on this planet are numbered. As I age, I rely less and less on the physical power of the muscles of my body and delight less and less in the mental abilities of my mind. I accept this life. Even though the days and years are short, they still contain infinite possibilities to grow and expand.

A Cold Autumn Day

The September wet snow is falling,
And the cold wraps itself around my thoughts
With this strange unusual chill,
      Out of time, out of season,
      Robbing me of sunshine.
My heart shivers in the cold grip of autumn.

I am aware that my mother and father,
My five brothers and three sisters,
Have already been planted in the frozen ground,
Beyond the reach of my eyes and ears,
Beyond the reach of a warm precious hug,
Leaving just a trace of their essence in my soul.
      I accept the shortness of life;
I accept that the days of autumn are numbered;
I accept that this snow will again blot out

The chance to frolic in the warm winds of summer.

A moment of silence.

As I feel the freshness of the cool autumn breeze,
I am aware that there is still something more,
Something beyond the clouds, the snow, the cold.
A warm feeling begins deep inside my soul,
And a quiet voice shouts out its forgotten message
That today is a gift to be wrestle from the arms of fate.
I rip it open in urgency before it evaporates.
I accept that I have only today, only this moment,
But this moment is all I need; this moment is all I desire.

Then I am aware of an even deeper feeling,
Deeper than I have ever felt before,
    Peeking through the frost and snow,
    Warming the depths of my soul.
A sliver of pure white light breaks out of its fragile shell,
Setting me free to see the glory all around me,
Setting me free to reach out and touch all those I love,
    An eternal gift to the present,
    A precious moment of ecstasy.

Week 4, Day 6
I Accept My Divine Nature

When I accept my own divine nature and begin to delight in my own presence, there is only joy. There is never a reason to be sad or depressed. I am never alone. I am part of the brotherhood of men and women who share a common vibration. All I have to do is still my mind and I can feel this sensation coursing through my nervous system. I recognize and accept that I am indeed an eternal, powerful being whose only purpose is to love.

Long Winter Nights

The days are short and the nights are long;
Living is not easy because there is too much striving,
Too much urgency to do something
That does not need to be done,
Too much urgency to be someone
I do not have to be.

The years are piling up,
One more season before three score and ten;
The seasons are all blending together,
And the winter tales are no longer worth repeating.
I sit her before my screen in the dark,
Searching for some important thing to say,
But I know deep inside

That everything has already been said.

The flowers are all tucked away beneath the ground;
The mulch has been laid to give them a cozy bed,
But the hope of a bright spring makes the toil worthwhile.

So meaning has to lie somewhere else,
            Somewhere within,
Somewhere where the sun never shines,
Some place where there is no darkness,
Some place where the ticking of the clock stops,
Some place where there is no need for sleep,
No need to rest and recuperate,
            Nothing to complain about,
            Nothing to brag about,
Just an endless parade of moments within moments,
Saturated with peace and joy,
            Where all is as it should be,
 Where there is no longer a need for DOING,
And just BEING is all there needs to be.

Week 4, Day 7
Accepting my Place in the Universe

Once I have accepted who I am, I can then accept life as it unravels around me. I can accept the trials that life has dealt me, knowing that they have made me into who I am. I am able to be conscious of just how precious these moments really are. Every day is a summer day.

Summer

(A Traditional Sonnet)

The sun, day by day, grows warmer, brighter,
Standing straighter, taller, in the noon day sky.
The winds whisper, somehow softer, sweeter,
Parting the days of spring and autumn with a sigh.
It is time to watch the blossoms burst again,
Releasing their life juices to expand and flow;
It is time to tend the soil and nurture new shoots,
That live to spread their new leaves and grow.
It is time to shake off winter's persistent cold,
Not to sit and weep for what might have been;
It is time for the old to be courageous and bold,
And embrace a new dream with a heart that is keen.
It is summer, my sweet love, a time to laugh and sing,
Time to greet the possibilities of all that life can bring.

Week 5
Forgiveness

There is so much beauty hidden in the desert. During my year in Arizona, I learned to enjoy the warmth of the sun, the persistent beauty of the vegetation, and the courage of the animals that dwelt there.

One day after hiking along desert paths steadily for five hot dry hours, I sat down on a rock and took in the dry harsh environment around me. I had another *aha moment*. I could see the truth of my situation. As my soul once again opened up to relive all the moments of perceived failure, shame, and guilt, I could see that I had done my best to survive in my own personal desert. I could see the courage of the little boy struggling to find his way alone in a hot dry world. I finally realized that the child was innocent; he was not to blame for not feeling loved. The young man was not to blame for having gay attractions. His struggle for sexual identity was not a disorder; it was a miraculous journey of courage and determination. The husband and father was not to blame for finally giving into uncontrollable compulsions and addictions that came from a mind and soul tortured by a Borderline Personality Disorder. In fact, he had done brilliantly just to hold himself together for thirty-three years, so that his children would have the kind of father he had never known.

Week 5, Day 1
Forgiving Myself

I had forgiven myself mentally, but the true healing took years of processing to become a reality. This type of forgiveness has to take place in the heart and soul and not just in the mind.   The beginning of true self-forgiveness came one morning during my meditation. I finally allowed the love of my Higher Self to pour into my mind and heart. It was like a warm moist wind blowing through my hot, dry soul.

I wept for hours for all the things that had been, had never been, and what might have been. I was finally free to forgive myself for all the mistakes I had made and for all the wrong I had done. Above all, I no longer had to take the blame for all the wrongs that had been done to me. I was finally free to leave my desert. There was no blame, no shame, no need for guilt. All just was. I was finally free to accept the whole and comforting meaning of forgiveness. I wiped the past clean and entered into a new world filled with warm moist winds and rich green life.

Ode to the Tree

Forgiveness comes like an October snowfall,
That quietly settles one flake at a time on the dead grass,
Covering the barren ground with pure soft white crystals,
A cool white shroud on summer's passionate past.

Feelings fall forgotten like frail dead leaves,
Without purpose and life beneath the white;
They are discarded bits of vanity and vitality,
Having fulfilled their purpose on the tree of life.

Yet, I remain in my state of shock like the tree,
Stripped of its drive, purpose, and ability to grow,
Thrusting my life blood back down into my roots,
Away from the cold November winds that blow.

But I still live, and I still feel, and I can still dream.
I know that those discarded feelings beneath the pain,
In time shall break down and nurture growth, new life,
When the warm spring sun shines overhead again.

And those feelings like last years living leaves,
Have contributed their substances to make me strong;
Their scars have become next year's branching points,
New life made ready for a new season with a new song.

Week 5, Day 2
Letting Go of the Hurt

The healing part of my journey was now complete. Those patterns and compulsions had all been changed through the miraculous healing power of forgiveness. The past was gone and I could now live in the present. I had peace of mind instead of generalized anxiety. I had joy instead of depression. I was a whole contented being instead of a broken soul with a personality disorder. And best of all, I had a renewed passion for living free of guilt, shame, and fear.

It Is Finished

All the prayers have been prayed; I have sung the last refrain;
The hurts have been washed away beneath the gently falling rain.
The pain, inflicted and received, has been burned, gone up in flame;
The grinding guilt, the demand to do it all over and over again,
Have all disintegrated in the vacant vapours of my cremated shame.

Gone, gone, gone they are all blissfully, thankfully gone, gone, gone.
I checked my pulse; it throbs still; my humble heart slowly beats on,
And all that remains is the peaceful purring of freeing forgiveness.
My soul is calm, no thoughts, no stress to greet the dawn.
This peace comes at last in the gentle hands of loving mindfulness.

My ego has died, given itself up gladly for the forgiveness of sin;
The resurrection of new life is birthing, breathing, bursting within.
The desire to enter into whatever heaven this new day has in store
Gasps its birth breath as the earth, moon, and stars begin to spin,
And all that will be cries out for more, and more, and more.

Where to from here? Back to Earth with no shelter from the past?
No, not back to Earth, but to a New World just beginning to be cast.
Come dance with me till our free spirits mind and soul redeem,
And our souls plead passionately that this moment will forever last,
For those of us who dare to live and breathe within the dream.

Week 5, Day 3
Refiring and Rewiring

In time, through spiritual practice, I was able to turn the dry dead desert of my life into a lush living garden. By daily opening up my mind to old regrets brought on by recurring reminders of past shame, I was able to gradually dissolve them. I let them surface again and again, one at a time, saw how each incident had changed me into the person I was now, and thanked the universe for each constructive hurt that I had endured. I then let the love from my heart flood my mind until I could feel a sense of pain mixed with joy. In the process, I built new neural circuits through the pleasure center of my brain changing the very fabric of my mind. It felt so good to gradually let all my past wounds go. My soul was now free to grow; and my heart was free to love.

The Changing Desert

I wander,
Barely breathing,
Into the desert of my mind.
No water,
No saving drops of moisture,
Just dry and silent faces
Carved on hot rocks
By my too hot mind,
Focused too long
On too hot thoughts.

Gentle rains fall on soft soil,
Nurturing luscious growth,
Bringing new life
To the images
Within my mind,
Continuously changing
The scenes of death before me
Into peaceful paths,
Where hope lingers,
And grows into reality.

Week 5, Day 4
Forgiving Others

Forgiveness is more than just saying, "I forgive you". I learned to forgive those who had contributed to my pain by digging deeper until I could see their own personal issues and struggles behind their actions and words. I simply revisualized the incident that had caused the hurt and walked it through to a positive conclusion. For some of these relationships, I was able to reconnect through phone calls, letters, or emails leading to a more complete feeling of forgiveness. But for most, it was just a simple process of visualizing the incident and resolving it in my mind. Then I imagined each memory as a package wrapped in love and carried on the wings of a dove back to the people I may have hurt or who may have hurt me.

My Little White Dove

Fly my little white dove,
I give you your freedom.
        Fly.
Fly free and joyously,
Released from the cage
In which I had imprisoned you.

Fly free my little friend.
        Fly.
Fly until you complete your journey.
Deliver this message of forgiveness
To the ones who receive my gift.
        Freedom.
They can now be free of me,
And I can now be free of them.

Then fly my little friend.
Search out your own destination.
Explore the open skies
Until your heart is full,
And your mind is free.

Then you alone can decide
Whether to return to me,
Or live beyond the fetters
Of unchained love.

Week 5, Day 5
Seeking Forgiveness from Past Loves

With those who were close to me, I had to see them once again to experience and feel the forgiveness. Where possible, I reconnected physically with them, eye to eye, heart to heart, leading to emotional and physical forgiveness, ending with a hug. I discovered that even though the physical bonds may have been damaged or even broken, there was still a remnant of shared love.

Goodbye to a Past Love

I shall always love you,
Mother of my children,
Now more than ever,
For now I see you as you are,
Not how I wanted you to be.

You are not the goddess
       I imagined;
You never were.
I just made you into her,
So that I could worship
Love and marriage,
My own husbandness,
My own fatherness.

You gave me what you could.
You sustained me
With your body and soul.
Now, too late,
I have the wisdom
To know you
And love you
Just as you really are,
And not how I wanted you to be.

Week 5, Day 6
Coming to Terms with Broken Parental Bonds

I visited my mother's grave site and sensed her presence and love in a way I had never sensed it in life. I forgave her for neglecting me. I was able to relive the cycle of emotional hurt and pain thus unravelling the events that had led to my borderline personality disorder. In the process of recognizing my mother's actions and the reasons behind them, I was able to truly forgive her, and I was able to stop blaming myself. I was not the cause and I was not a victim. There was no blame. There was no shame. There was only love.

Good-Bye Mom

I shall always love and cherish you, Mom,
Now more than ever,
For now I see you as you are,
Not how I wanted you to be.
I had to make you perfect,
For you were my security.
But you were broken;
You lost your mother, your father,
Your husband, two of your daughters.
You gave me what you could.
You sustained me in your brokenness,

I thank you for giving me strength to live,
For setting me on my own path
To discover what it means to be a parent,
So I could break the cycle,
So I could provide a loving father
For my own children,
Determined to keep on giving
When there was nothing left to give,
So they could grow up to be
Contented whole human beings
Who are the product of your love and mine.

Week 5, Day 7
Moving On

I even forgave the god I had created. But like in forgiveness of others, it was not really forgiveness. It was just a decision to clean up the past, search for clarity and understanding, and make a new beginning. I set aside the judgmental god I had created, the one that could forgive me when I could not forgive myself. I set aside the illusion of the Father I never had, that imaginary source of love and understanding who could show me how to be a good father. Once my mind was free of the god-patterns of the past, I realized there was no need to do penance for mind-created sin. This revelation opened up the world of new possibilities where I was intimately connected to the universal presence where there was no judgement, therefore no need for guilt. I was free to experience whatever I wanted to experience. So along with Dr. Martin Luther King I can now truly say, *"thank god, I am free at last"*.

Moving On

I shall always love and cherish you,
Spirit of Love,
Now more than ever,
For now I see you as you are,
Not how I wanted you to be.
You are not the judge and prosecutor,
The being I created to forgive myself,

To bury my guilt, and erase my shame.
You are not the father I never had,
The shoulder to lean on and cry on,
  The voice of wisdom,
  The path to follow,
When all was just confusion and delusion.

Now I can see you for who you really are.
You are the spirit of love
That is always there to open up
The floodgates of the universe,
Through a thought, a touch,
  A moment of peace.
Now that I know I am loved by you,
I can love myself and say:

"I shall always love you, Lawrence,
Now more than ever,
For now I see you as you are;
You are not the person I thought you were,
Or how I desperately wanted you to be.
You are not the loathsome creature I imagined.

  You never were."

Part 2
The Centering Virtues

Centering is a spiritual term defining a process whereby we become centered or balanced. This place exists within the space and purpose provided by our Higher Self which balances the life force from the gut, the hopes and fears from the mind, the desire to love and be loved from the heart, and our source of knowing and being from our soul. Being centered is having a mind state where the mind let's go and refers to the heart and soul. It is a mental and spiritual state to come back to when life's challenges and emotions push us off balance. For our purposes, I have composed this definition:

Centering is a state of spiritual and physical being that brings inner peace and joy regardless of the situation and circumstances of our physical life.

I have identified five qualities that will help us stay centered. They are:

- Gratitude
- Appreciation
- Contentment
- Fortitude
- Gentleness

Week 6
Gratitude

Gratitude is our response to kindness, gifts, and other acts of generosity from others. It is the opposite of blame and regret. Scientifically, it has been demonstrated that gratitude results in less stress and more satisfaction with our lives. We have lower levels of anxiety and depression. We tend to cope with life through positive responses rather than negative. We show a greater appreciation for life. We seek wholesome relationships with others. We even sleep better. We live longer and happier lives. There is so much to be thankful for.

Week 6, Day 1
Gratitude for my Mother

My mother had an extremely hard life. She experienced the feeling of helplessness as two of her children died before her eyes, one in infancy and one in childhood. Her husband left her to raise the eight remaining children by herself. Somehow, she miraculously managed to hold herself and her family together and raised her children the best way she knew how. I was the "illegitimate" and ninth baby of the family.

When I was going through therapy, my team of a psychiatrist and four therapists wanted me to get in touch with my emotions which had been shut down through depression. They forced me to see that as a child I had been neglected by my mother and raised by my older siblings resulting in a Borderline Personality Disorder that I had had to live with for the rest of my life.

The therapists wanted me to show anger at my mother. How could I? She had done the best she could with impossible circumstances. As I was awakening spiritually, rather than anger, blame, and regret, I reacted with admiration, love, and gratitude.

Mom

Thank you Mom, you gave me life,
An accident perhaps,
Another inconvenient child to feed,
Another heart to nurture when your ability to love
Had been destroyed by life's circumstances.

You gave what you could.

At times in my darkest hours,
I wished I had never been born,
And I forgot the sacrifice you made to give me life.
I tried to pass on my self-hate to you but could not.
And in the process of refusing to blame you,
I came to the point
Where I no longer had to blame myself.

It was what it was.

It is what it is.

My eyes were opened.
I watched you raise me and give me a chance to live,
Rather than abort me or abandon me
To people and circumstances beyond your control.
You continued to give me life,
A chance to live and learn for myself
That I have the same power to survive that you had.

You gave me the power to get up in the morning,
And do the best I could with what I had been given,
The power to offer unconditional love
      To my own children
      When I could not love myself.
In the hours of life and gratitude that followed,
I am thankful that you chose to see life through,
And in the process chose to see me through.

Thank you mom for being you,
For never giving up,
For cherishing life over death,
For finding help from a higher power
      When you felt helpless,
For keeping your feet moving forward
      When you felt hopeless,
Never giving in to feelings of self-blame,
Choosing to live one day at a time,
      One moment at a time.

Thank you mom for showing me the way.

Week 6, Day 2
Gratitude to My Brothers and Sisters

I grew up as the seventh son, the youngest of nine, in a single parent family. I was six years younger than Ivan, my closest brother. Special thanks to you, Ivan, for letting me tag along with you and your older friends, for providing a home for me during my first three years of university in Edmonton, and for just being my closest friend during my first years of adulthood. When I look back at those years now as a conscious being, I can see that life was not easy for you, but you gave me what could, unselfishly and lovingly.

Special thanks to you, Victor, my older brother, who took it upon yourself to be the dad I never had during my childhood and early teen years, for buying all my sports equipment and attending all my games. I could tell you were proud of my athletic achievements which kept me out of trouble when my childhood friends all fell by the wayside.

And a special thanks to you, my two sisters, for you, Ramona, who quit school at thirteen to raise your baby brother, and you, Jean, for being the matriarch of the family during most of my adult years.

And finally, a special thank you to you, Garry, for being my last remaining brother, and my dear friend, during our twilight years.

Flesh and Blood

Thank you my brothers and sisters,
So close, yet so far apart,
Each of us on our own island,
Trying to withstand the waves of life's cruelties,
But seldom sharing inner wounds and feelings,
Holding them back until the anger exploded,
Breaking the levees of emotion,
Spilling the boiling rage on those near,
Yet never holding grudges,
Never having to say "I'm sorry".

Family, compelled by circumstances,
To pull together with no father,
And an emotionally absent mother,
Never looking for excuses to quit,
Never looking for the easy way out
Through drugs or alcohol,
Just rolling up your sleeves and pitching in,
Working and sharing paychecks with the family.

Thank you for holding my babies,
And loving them as your own,
For being there without judgement
When my life came apart,
For accepting without question
My sexual orientation.

Most of you are gone now,
Just one brother and one sister left,
But you are not forgotten.
You live still in my thoughts and memories;
You are a part of me,
A part of the man I am now,
And a part of the man I will always be.

Week 6, Day 3
Gratitude to my Teachers and Mentors

When I look back at my childhood and young adult days, there were so many people who took the time to give this young lad a helping hand. I am especially grateful to the fathers of St. Thomas College who got me through my teen years in one piece. Most of you are gone now, but your memories and words of life live on.

Special thanks to you, Father Herman, my French teacher, you taught me never to shirk my responsibilities and to make sure I always handed in my assignments on time by leaning your two hundred and fifty pound six foot six frame on my sagging shoulder and then pulling me up by the hair on the back of my neck until I had to stand on my chair and explain why I had not completed my homework. But you did it with a touch of love and humor.

Special thanks to you, Father Stang, my Latin teacher, my principal and golf buddy. You accepted all my lame excuses for being late when I had stopped for one more game of pool before returning for afternoon classes.

A special thanks to you, Father Pius Seiben, my counsellor and friend, you taught me to believe in myself. You performed my marriage ceremony, joining a Catholic and a protestant, in spite of the objections and prejudice from both sides, reminding everyone that marriage is sacred because it is an act of unconditional love.

Thank You to All My Teachers

Thank you to all my teachers,
Who saw the intelligence and potential
In the little boy from a broken home,
Who saw gifts and talents
Instead of anger and shame,
And showed a clear path to a bright future.

Thank you to those teachers
Who went past being a teacher
And became my mentors,
Taking upon yourselves the responsibility
To bring the raw material into a refined quality,
Seeing the possibilities in the eyes of a child,
For not letting me be satisfied with mediocrity,
But forcing me into the realm of excellence,
And my rightful place in the sun.

Thank you to you teachers
Who saw not only a student,
But a kindred spirit,
And took the time to become my friend,
Stopping in the hallways to engage me,
Not in small talk, but in big talk,
About my hopes and dreams,
About my sorrows and disappointments.

Thank you, all of you,
For the extra time you spent,
Way beyond the call of duty,
Giving without any hope of receiving,
Just because you cared.

Week 6, Day 4
Gratitude to the Women Who Have Loved Me

Through a life of callousness, unconscious behavior, and heartbreak, I have finally learned the meaning of intimate love. I have learned to love through the shared experiences of raising a family, a codependency relationship where we both strived to overcome depression and mental disorders, and a cohabitation where we both needed to be anchored instead of isolated. In each case, I did truly love, but the level and dimension of that love varied.

Perhaps my so-called love failures were not failures at all. I learned from my intimate relationships that my brokenness could not be fixed by leaning on someone else. In the process, I have learned there is no guilt, there is no blame, all just is. In fact, once I could accept that relationships were not necessarily designed to be forever, that we are not necessarily bonded till death like the cooing doves, I was able to move from relationship to relationship learning and expanding.

I am now married to a beautiful conscious woman. I have come to realize that what remains is myself, my life purpose, and a kindred spirit to share in an intimate, conscious, and joyous relationship. The role of relationship is for each of us to assist the other in understanding our purpose, working together to support each other on each other's path to self-actualization, and to simply enjoy our passions for the pure joy and pleasure of intimacy.

Partnership

We are in this together,
    You and I,
Fine-honed instruments,
Holding tune in time and adversity
While being played by a higher power.

We are two souls come together,
Intertwined in a common cause
By a force greater than you and I,
A force that we have created,
And by a force that has created us,
Melding our energies together
In a common cause.

We help each other grow and expand
To be yet more than we were,
And yet more than we are now,
Two souls vibrating in harmony,
Two sources of infinite energy
    Combining in purpose,
So that we can create a space in time
Where we can yield the power
To melt frozen hearts,
And to move mountains.

And so we thrive,
Putting aside the voices that would say
We are not good enough to make a difference,
Too fragile to hold love's overflowing energy,
Too weak to run the race to the finish line.
But we are emboldened by desire,
Enlivened with passion,
Wielding the power of purpose,
To share a piece of our essence with each other,
And then supporting each other
In our desire to share our essence with others,
A divine energy of two,
Infinitely more than the power of one.

Week 6, Day 5
Gratitude to my Children

One of the chief ways to achieve my main purpose, which is to expand and grow, was to have and nurture my children. I love them unconditionally, and now that they are adults, they in turn love me unconditionally. By being loved unconditionally by my children, I have finally learned to love myself unconditionally.

As my children grew into adults, I saw them mature into pure beings, separate from me, but yet bonded and connected. Through awareness of this bonded love, I have become aware of the bond that I share with nature and other human beings. I have learned to love in all things. I have developed and nurtured a love energy that will propel me into eternity.

My Children

My Children,
Flesh of my flesh, blood of my blood,
Thank you for teaching me how to be a father
When I had no father to show me the way.

So much I gave,
And in giving so much,
I received so much from you.

Love,
So much love,
So much caring,
So much hoping.

So much striving to be the best I could be,
So that you could be the best you could be.
So much sadness when you were sad,
So much joy when you were happy,
Until my eyes filled with tears,
And my heart overflowed with pride.

Thank you for teaching me,
That it is my responsibility to love unconditionally,
Even when it hurts, even when I could not love myself,
Even when the world stopped loving me,
For teaching me to love just for the sake of love,
Just because you were you
And just because I am your father.

As you have become adults with children of your own,
        Thank you for still being my friend.
As we have all grown older and wiser,
        Thank you for that hug
That says you understand now the sacrifices I made.
I am proud with a father's pride,
That you too understand the meaning of unconditional love,
        And now give it back to me.

Week 6, Day 6
Gratitude to My Students and Readers

I officially retired from educational psychology fifteen years ago, but I could not stay retired. I still teach advanced placement psychology on-line to students who are homebound for physical or emotional reasons. Beyond that, I still blog about mental wellness and write books of poetry that are not just for artistic expression but are what I call *Poetry with a Purpose*. I continue to get positive feedback from my students and subscribers encouraging me to keep giving my message.

But more than that, I feel that this message has become clearer and more powerful as I have grown professionally as a poet and as a person. I cannot quit now just when the going gets going. I believe I have been given a purpose by the universe to enlighten and inspire my fellow human beings to become aware of just how beautiful and powerful they can be.

Poetry

I am thankful that I am a poet.
I create and share my art,
Just because I have to,
To massage the ache in my heart.

Thank you brothers and sisters, my family,
Who read what I write and share my dreams,
Who strive to read between the lines
And discover that life is not way it seems.

Thank you readers who have taken the time
To understand and see the possibilities,
To translate my insights into your thoughts,
And apply my poems to create a life of probabilities.

Thank you lovers of poetry,
Who see beyond the heartache and the strife,
Who dare to expose your heart and soul,
And reach for the deeper dimensions of life.

Week 6, Day 7
Gratitude – Giving Thanks to the Giver of Life

Above all, I am thankful for the life force that is in me and for the giver of life which is nameless and beyond the boundaries of religion. But I am also truly thankful for the sincere and compassionate pastors and priests who have led me deeper and deeper into the knowledge that what I perceive as my higher power is so much more than just a higher power. It is the universal consciousness, the energy that is at the center of thought, creativity, and love. In essence, I now worship love and life itself, the life which flows through me, and the love which I can pass on to my fellow man.

Thank You for Life

I give thanks to the source of life,
Perhaps an intelligence that is life itself.
The mystery that the profits and mystics
Attempt to unravel, is no mystery at all.

It just is
And I just am.

I am continuously and consciously
With and in the I Am,
And so I have become the I Am
And the I Am has become Me.

My soul exists in and as the center of life,
I am the creator of my own purpose,
I am the savior of my own soul,
I choose to believe in myself,
I choose to believe in community of SELFS,
And in the essence of life itself,

Of which I am a part
And which is a part of me.

Week 7
Appreciation

Gratitude is thankfulness for what someone has done, but appreciation is the acceptance and love of life as it is. The practice of appreciation begins in the heart, becomes a light in our eyes, and travels onto our face with a smile. It is the practice of looking for the good in life, in others, and in ourselves. It can be a hot cup of coffee on a cold day, a smile shared with a stranger, or a dinner shared with friends or family. When these things happen, our soul responds with positive vibrations which flow to our heart and into our mind and body. As in the case of gratitude, appreciation is related to the gentle emotions that keep our heart centered and our mind at peace. We live longer and love better, thus creating positive energies to pass on to others. When we appreciate life, it becomes a mirror to our soul so that we can reflect to others the joys of living a conscious life.

Week 7, Day 1
Appreciation for the Gifts of Nature

Love of nature is the healing substance of my Higher Self. My mind goes quiet and just lets my body experience sensations through my senses. My body absorbs vibrations of harmony from nature which bring peace and contentment to my mind, a love response from my heart, and a feeling of joy to my soul.

Nature's Gifts

I appreciate nature's gifts.
I see with my heart
All the treasures given by mother Earth:

> The morning sun that brings in a new day,
> The flowers that bloom in my garden,
> The rabbits, and even the raccoons,
> That frequent my yard,
> The eagles that fly overhead
> Casting a shadow on my lawn,
> The plaintive cries of the seagulls,
> The honking of the geese,
> And the haunting sounds of the loons
> That echo across Baynes Sound.

And I appreciate these eyes that see all,
This mind that remembers and creates,
And this heart that feels and loves.

Week 7, Day2
I Appreciate the Place I Call Home

It is important for me to appreciate where I live. Whether it is an apartment in an inner city or a country estate, it is the place where I can unwind and be myself. It has the furniture that I have carefully selected and a few objects that trigger pleasant memories that give me a sense of peace and belonging. It contains my photographs and mementos of a life lived.

However, while being contented in my mind, I have also wished to find a place that meets the needs of my soul. To me that is my present home in Baynes Sound. It feels like I have finally come home after a lifetime of wandering. I can honestly say that my body, mind, and soul are now content. I appreciate where I live now, not just because it is my home, but because it harmonizes with the energies of my soul.

Baynes Sound

As I stand here on my deck in mindful meditation,
My eyes open with wonder, my mind silent with awe,
I gaze at the space between Denman Island and Deep Bay,
The border between Baynes Sound and the Salish Sea,
And my heart fills with joy and my soul with knowing,
That this is a small piece of heaven, a glimpse of eternity.

The May sunrise grows from a red ribbon on the horizon,
To a blossom of pinks and reds reflecting from sky to sea.
I sense the flowing currents shifting with the peaceful tides,
And deep inside where my body ends and my soul begins,
  I breathe deeply, refreshing my spirit,
  Knowing that I have yet one more day
To thank the gods that be that I live where I live.

Week 7, Day 3
I Appreciate Canada

This dear country of Canada is an amazing place. I have lived in five of the ten provinces and loved each of them for their unique contributions to the life force within my soul. I grew up on the prairies with the wide open skies and the miles of golden wheat fields swaying in the ever present prairie winds. I spent two years in Northern Manitoba in the vast Canadian Shield surrounded by stunted evergreen forests and a complex pattern of lakes and rivers connecting to the Arctic Ocean. I lived and worked for twenty years in Alberta, which was at that time my place for professional growth and where I watched my children grow up and establish themselves as compassionate human beings. I spent four years on Cape Breton Island on the shores of Lac Bras d'Or, an inland sea that cut into my heart and soul. And now in my later years, I have settled on Vancouver Island, a blend of old growth forest, mountains, and the ever-present Salish Sea. Each of these places have contributed what I needed at that specific point in time, so that I could grow and expand into the person I have become.

In spite of the flaws of our political and economic system, I still feel a oneness with the conscious souls of this precious land: the farmers of the prairies, the fishermen of the east and west coasts, the people who have brought their cultures with them from distant lands, and especially the indigenous people with whom I share a spiritual connection with the land.

Canada

I hear the drums of the people who first came to this land,
And I am compelled to dance their dances
In the costumes of the creature spirits,
From the prairie chicken of the prairies,
To the eagle and the raven of the West Coast.
As they all bring their gifts of generosity, harmony, and peace,
The differences between us disappear in the spirit of oneness,
Oneness with nature, the sky, the Earth, and each other.
They become a part of me and I become a part of them.
We are one people, one heart that beats with one rhythm.

But somewhere we forgot our partnership
With the people of the land;
And we destroyed the great coastal forests,
Setting aside what remained into tree museums,
A rarity, just a relic of the sacred, an oddity for tourists.
And we kept dipping our nets greedily into the abundant seas
Until the cod and herring were almost gone,
And the salmon that fed on the herring began to disappear,
And the orcas that fed on the salmon threatened extinction.
> We ignored the sacred messages
> Of harmony, generosity, and community.
> We lost ourselves in the noise
> Of jackhammers, saws, and machinery.
> We became a part of the chaos
> And the chaos became a part of us.

But it is not too late. I still believe in the power of "us";
     We are still one people;
     We can still mourn our loss with one heart.
     We can still roll up our sleeves,
     And learn once again
To cherish the sound of the sacred waters,
And bow our heads when we hear the soft whispers
Of the wind through the evergreens.
We can learn to be awed
By the high-pitched song of the eagles;
We can learn to honour the forest,
The ground and the seas that give us life;
And we can share our sorrows, wealth, and gifts,
     In one daily celebration of life,
     In one great Canadian potlatch,
Giving each other our special talents and gifts.

We can learn to speak once again with one voice,
     And feel the beat of one heart,
         For we are Canada;
         We are one.

Week 7, Day 4
I Appreciate my Body

The spiritual purpose of this body is to sense and feel. I have a physical power that originates in my heart and flows through my gut and brain. When under the influence of my Higher Self, my brain can choose what to sense, perceive, and think. Above all, I have spiritual, mental, and physical energies that intertwine to create me, the person inside this body. This makes me into an amazing being with the power to create any life I choose to live. It all starts when my body absorbs and creates feelings for my heart to love and my soul to enjoy.

Feeling Powerful

The blood is flowing again today
Into all the soft spots,
Bringing light to the darkness,
Bringing heat to my cold thoughts.

I am alive again,
Rushing towards I know not what,
Just believing the goal will be good,
And if not, the journey will be worth the ride.

Feeling the power,
Not to climb mountains,
But to absorb them into my being,
To become one with them,
To master their essence.
Feeling the power,
To walk on the sea,
And to explore its depths,
To make it bend to my wishes,
To feel the comfort of the waves.

Feeling the power,
Like I have something to share,
To bring the world to its knees,
To bring salvation to my tired soul,
To bring comfort to the brotherhood of poets.

Week 7, Day 5
I appreciate My Mind

In spiritual circles, my mind, or ego, has been labelled as the negative part of my being, whereas my soul is the positive. I beg to disagree. The ego is me, my identity, the 'me' that lives and works and plays in this time and space of being I call life.

In the physical reality, I am my orbitofrontal cortex (OFC), the administrator from the left side, and my sense of being in time and space on the right, combined with the sensory receptors and processors, and the memories of past experiences. The OFC takes in new information and combines it with the old to create and change mind states. This combination of neural pathways, or mind states, become my thoughts when my OFC approaches a problem that needs to be solved. In reality this combination of my mind states and my OFC is the mental/emotional/physical me.

My mind has to be treasured for what it is, but it has its limitations. It must be centered with my heart and soul to create my sense of being beyond time and space.

My Mind

I appreciate my mind,
The bad boy of my family;
My body, heart, and soul would be lost without it.
It takes what my eyes see and my ears hear,
And melts these sensations into past memories,
And mingles them with the centers of my emotions,
The things I fear and the things I love,
And creates these amazing feelings,
That feed my soul and fill my heart.

I appreciate my logical mind,
That sees what can be and asks why not,
Where the impossible
Suddenly becomes the possible,
As my mind sets out to take my dream
To the place where dreams become reality.
Then my mind sets a path,
Step by step ever closer to the goal.
And then the great "aha",
As it all comes together,
And the pleasure center of my brain
Lights up with a high that itself creates,
A feeling of power,
A belief that I am invincible.

I appreciate my creative mind,
That envisions images that my hands can recreate
Through a mixture of oils or water colors
Arranged mystically on a white canvas,
So that my heart and soul can see and feel itself,
That creates words out of thoughts
That can tell stories about people
That exist first in the mind of the writer,
And then again in the mind of the reader,
That creates poems out of an infinite possibility of images,
Then adds tones and melodies of sounds and feelings
That hold up a mirror where my mind can see itself,
And understand the mysteries of why it exists.

I appreciate my intuitive mind,
That creates a mindset absent of any gestalt,
Where it rests and the soul begins,
A schema of all the schemas,
A state of mindlessness that we call mindfulness,
Where all is at rest except all the sensations
That are allowed to play each in turn and all at once.

I appreciate that my mind understands
That there must be an external presence,
Where a feeling of oneness can exist
With all things that live and have lived,
That bows to the soul to reveal the mystery,

            That the I Am lives in ME.

Week 7 Day 6
I Appreciate My Heart

My heart is the mystical and the physical, the sensuous and the ethereal. As my physical heart pumps blood to all the cells of my body, keeping them alive and forming a river of essence that holds them all together, my spiritual heart arises out of the physical, sharing my life energy, my essence, with the essence of all living things. It is the creative power of my soul; it is the core of my being. It is the desire to create and to procreate and then to love and nurture new life.

Beat on My Heart

Beat on my heart,
Forever and forever,
Beat on.

You are the mystery of mysteries;
You are the ME in me,
The eternal in the temporal,
The infinite in the finite.

Beat on my heart;
Sing your songs,
Write your poems,
Paint the pictures
Of a mind lost in a sea of woe,
Give my mind stability in the chaos,
Give my life meaning
Where there is no meaning.

Beat on my heart.
Be my ability to connect with all,
With one,
With the one I choose to love now,
In this moment of moments.

Beat on my heart;
Let love flow from the ME in me
To the YOU in you,
And into the ALL in all.

Beat on my heart
Be YOU,
Be ME,
Be the heartbeat within me.
Be the heartbeat of the universe,
Be the ALL in all.

Beat on my heart,
Forever and forever,
Beat on.

Week 7 Day 7
I Appreciate My Soul

I appreciate my soul, my spirit, my life energy, the eternal presence in the temporal me. Together with my heart, which is the physical portion of my eternal being, they create my ability to live a life beyond the limits of body and mind. This is a world of love for life, for all living things, and for those eternal souls that share this life with me. I appreciate that I am more than my eyes can see and more than my mind can understand. I am the I AM in my soul.

Full

The double life, the two sides to the coin,
The proverbial glass that is half full or half empty,
Are all excuses of my tired mind;
The reality is kinder, softer, and sweeter.

Even though the reality perceived by my mind
Is sometimes hard to bear and it appears at times
That the glass is completely empty,
All I have to do is close my eyes,
And enter into the reality of my soul.

Here the glass is always full and overflowing.
Soon the overflow from the inside glass
Flows down into the outside glass,
Until it too is full and overflowing.

Then I open my eyes and all that was hidden before
Is now revealed to the eyes within my soul,
And I can see the beauty of my hidden world,
And watch the illusions and delusions dissolve
And evaporate into the clearing skies.

Week 8
Contentment

Contentment is a state of happiness and satisfaction with who we are and what we do. True contentment is freedom from want and desire. If we are content, we are no longer dependent on material goods. We focus on finding and keeping positive feelings and letting go of the negative. If we are content, we can be alone and be perfectly happy. It is a feeling of safety and comfort, an overwhelming sense of satisfaction with life. Contentment is a feeling of belonging in community with other conscious souls. It is a feeling of being one with the source of life and love. We have opened our hearts, minds, and souls to the beauty and synchronicity of the world in us and around us.

Week 8, Day 1
The Centre of Contentment

My key to contentment is to find that quiet spot at the center of my being where I seem to float in time and space free of any anxious thought. Once I have found it, I can lock it into my memory as a mind state. Once I have locked it in, it is forever mine to visit whenever the world seems to be too much to bear. It is my place of *being* where my heart and soul take over and my mind or state of *doing* is put to rest. My quiet spot is my physical and spiritual sanctuary, my centre of contentment.

The Quiet Spot

There is a quiet spot hidden is a secret place,
That cannot be reached by searching or striving.
There is gold here that is beyond the riches of kings,
That cannot, and must not, be mined, saved, or spent.
There is peace there that can be easily shattered,
The tighter you hold it, the faster it crumbles.
There is contentment there that can only be experienced
One moment at a time, but each moment is timeless.

It is here that I find the answers to all my questions,
Where stresses of the world meet the desires of my heart,
Where earth meets sky and flowers always bloom,
Where the eagles majestically soar and robins joyfully sing,
Where the struggles of life and death melt and fade away,
Leaving just a seed that births and nurtures new life.

There is a place inside me that has been built by my soul,
A place of peace where I am fully aware of my own being,
Where I find the courage to live another day,
And to spread the joy of living to everyone I meet.

Week 8, Day 2
Content with my Emotions

Contentment has not come easy for me; I have to work at it. Through my connection with my Higher Self, I have learned to live with my anxiety disorder. Now I can consciously shut down my anxieties and quiet my negative emotions. There is no more fear, no more anger, no more shame. All just is. I can shut them all down anytime I feel their presence. I simply enter into my quiet spot and my contentment is something I can consciously feel and treasure.

At Peace with My Emotions

Having fought the wars to control my mind,
Of having my existence authenticated by others,
My worth validated by followers and likes,
Of having endured the anxieties of competing,
Thrusting my self-worth before the masses
In fear and in hope of being recognized,
I have made up my mind
To no longer worship the gods
Of popularity and prosperity.
I choose to worship the god within,
Who lives to bestow peace and contentment
To my broken heart and my tired mind.

I am content.

The world has stopping spinning wildly,
Settling into its slow and steady pace
Of living one day at a time,
One moment at a time.
I recognize the ME in the toil,
And tell myself it's okay just to be ME.
I lean into the comfort of the breeze on my face,
The wind whispering through the spruce trees
That surround my humble abode.
I recognize the voice of my soul
Silently speaking behind my mind.

       I am content.

My emotions no longer run wild
In the playground of my mind,
But have come to rest
Below the fresh-leaved maple trees,
That have learned to stay rooted
In one place and grow.
I too have learned to stay rooted
In the comforts of my soul,
No longer longing to venture out
And risk the futility of expanding
Without being grounded,
So that the storm winds that shake my foundation
No longer hold any power over me.
I am rooted in one place in peace.

       I am content.

Week 8, Day 3
Content with Time and Place

Being content means there is no need to make sense of my past and no striving to assure that my needs will be met in the future. The past was difficult to deal with, mainly because I had a Borderline Personality Disorder and an anxiety disorder that went along with it. That meant that most of my past experiences were linked to the negative emotions of fear, anger, and shame. That combination of memories and emotions created powerful mind states or paradigms which had ruled my life.

But it has also proved to be a blessing. It has taught me to recognize the triggers in my physical and social-emotional environments and to reroute them from negative feelings to positive feelings. I can now express gratitude for the experiences because they have made me into the person I can now love and appreciate. I realize now that all sources of anxiety in the past were opportunities to learn be thankful and content within myself in the now.

Goodbye to the Past

I have said goodbye to the past,
Those moments of regret can no longer hold me back.
Even though the shame mechanism in my brain
Lights up with every passing sensation,
Determined to reactivate the memories of my mind,

Those mind states that contain past failures and shame,
They no longer have any power to hold and enfold me.
I simply consciously interrupt and reroute the circuitry
Through my smile and my field of knowing
That all is okay in my present world.

I have stopped fighting those voices
That keep saying it all is hopeless,
That it is time to lie down and give up.
They are now redirected to my soul
That says:

>"There is no need to feel tired;
>There is no past; there is no future;
>There is only today; there is only this moment
>There is only peace; there is only joy,
>There is only love, for myself and for life."

My world has been reduced to a single thought,
To enjoy the sensations of life
That are there to be savoured,
So I can smile and say,

>"It is what it is.
>I am at peace,
>I have today to celebrate
>The joy of being alive,
>The joy of being me"

Week 8 Day 4
Contentment is Living in the Moment

As I get older, one of the greatest sources of stress is wanting to be assured that my life has meaning and purpose. But none of this really matters. The key is to enjoy life now just for what it is, with no thoughts of an afterlife, no thoughts about meaning and purpose. My purpose is simply to accept one day at a time as a gift from the universe. If I align my energies with the life flow from the universe, all things will work together for my own gratification and for the work I do to bring peace and contentment to others. If an afterlife happens, great; if not, it's been a hell of a good ride.

Just Human

I am content
To know that I am human,
 Just human,
With just this limited mind,
With just this fragile body,
With just these few days lived,
With just these last few days left to live.

I am content
To see these days pass swiftly,
Taking me beyond the boundaries of time,
Not knowing if my essence will survive,
Or just dissipate into thoughtless energy.

I am content
Because I have embraced life.
I have shared my breath with these ancient trees,
And watched and felt the sunrise on the Salish Sea,
As a surge of pure golden energy has engulfed my body,
So that I can create and experience the harmony of being
Within my body, mind, and soul and with all living things.

I am content
Because I have lived this life to the fullest,
Daring to be me and to dream my own dreams,
To create my own reality, and live my own life,
To forge my own path through the chasms of chaos,
And to dare to follow in my own footsteps.

I am content,
Because I have felt the breath of life
Stir the desires and passions of my body;
I have lived to create and to procreate,
And to pass on all that is me and in me
To those who have followed,
To those whom I love.

I am content
Because I have passed on my essence
To my sons and my daughters,
And through them to each and every generation
That will follow in our footsteps.

I am content
Because I have passed on the essence of my mind
Through these humble thoughts and images
That I have put on paper and bound into books,
So that someone, somewhere,
    Will see what I see,
    Think what I think,
    And feel what I feel.

I am content
Because I know I have lived and fulfilled my life purpose.
I have cherished the essence of this life that is ME.
I have shared this life with all living things.
I have shared my soul with my fellow man,
And above all I have shared my heart
With those whom I have loved,
A cherished few who have known the real ME,
    And loved me.

Week 8, Day 5
The Difference Between Wants and Needs

I have learned the difference between wants and needs. All my physical needs are taken care of. I have a pension that meets my need for a roof over my head and bread on my table. My social needs are met through my soul mate, my family, friends, and acquaintances in my community. My spiritual needs became a thing of the past the moment I became conscious of the universal presence and realized that I am a beautiful and powerful human being.

My wants? I have none. I have all I want and they are all simple things that are all free, free for my mind and soul to accept, embrace, and enjoy. Life is simple. I have no desire for material things. I have no desire to journey to distant places. I have the ocean to greet me each morning and the forest paths just a step away.

Free to Be Me

I am free at last,
Free from the tyranny of possessions,
For I have five pairs of shoes and a drawer full of socks;
Free from the desire to travel to places I have never been,
For I have lived in five provinces in my beloved Canada,
And experienced living in the cultures on three continents.

I am free from the desires to be accepted and loved,
For I have accepted myself and love myself,
And I am accepted and loved by my soul-mate,
By my friends and family.

I am free of the need to produce a product
That is needed and shared with my community,
For I have lived and worked and played with passion.

I am free from the religion of thoughts of an afterlife,
Because I am content with the life I live.

I am free just to be me,
To watch the days drift by.
I am free to feel the ocean breeze on my hands and face,
To walk the familiar paths through my friends the trees.
I am free to set aside my mind long enough to breathe.
I am free to stop at any moment in time
To feel my soul hum with contentment,
And know that I am all I need and love is all I want.

Week 8, Day 6
Content with my Life Work

The key to living a life of contentment is to cease striving to be something I am not, and to be content knowing and sharing my gifts and talents. I have found contentment through my poetry. These thoughts, feelings, and words have been given to me as I have calmed my mind and opened my heart and soul to the universal presence of life and love. They are an offering that I give freely and lovingly to my fellow human beings. Even if I can help just one someone love themselves and love this life just a little bit more, it will all have been worth it. I will be content that I have done my part in the progress of humankind.

Poetry

These days lie fallow
Beneath the stubble
Of last year's field of green.
The moments have passed
Beyond the reach of memories,
And I wait for the new spring sun to shine,
New growth, new thoughts,
To quicken my tired mind.

The flowers still bloom,
And the moments still pass
One by one into infinity,
And my thoughts still emerge
From this tired brain,
Begging to be put into words,
And words into stanzas,
To be shared with one someone,
Somewhere, somehow,
A connection between two minds,
A connection between two souls.

And all I have been is enough,
All the dreams I have dreamt are sufficient;
My thoughts are worth repeating,
My poems worth sharing.
Some have listened,
And more will listen,
And some will go beyond listening,
And begin to care.

I will be able to rest
And say I have done enough,
And pass quietly into eternity.

Week 8, Day 7
Contentment With Living and Aging

I am at peace with the process of living and aging. I will not say "living and dying" because I do not believe I will die. I am aging graciously. I take good care of my body and my mind. I am dedicated to the growth of my soul. I am like the butterfly that enters into a cocoon where I will be transformed from a caterpillar who crawls along the Earth to a being of light who sails on into the open skies. Life is about transforming into a being of pure divine love-based energy.

My Transformation

All is as it should be.
The days are shorter,
And the nights are getting longer.
The shadows disappear
Into their dark world,
And my mind is at peace
        With itself.

The moments are here to be savoured
Like fine wine during a good meal;
And I have tasted all the flavors of life.

I am content.

My hopes no longer draw me
Kicking and screaming,
But quietly beckon,
Revealing themselves as truths
That need to be understood and accepted
As the wisdom of another dimension
That has crossed over
To the world in which I live.

I am content.

Week Nine
Fortitude

Fortitude refers to strength in the face of adversity or difficulty. It comes from the Latin word *fortitudo*, meaning "strength." It includes such qualities as courage, strength of mind, strength of character, toughness of spirit, firmness of purpose, resilience, and stout-heartedness. It is composed of mental, emotional, and spiritual powers or reserves which allow us to stand firm and fight courageously for what we believe. Through fortitude, we are able to see the entire problem and make the right decisions based on the desires of our heart and the wisdom of our soul. Fortitude gives us the strength to pursue and live a conscious life, a life of purpose and power.

Week Nine, Day 1
Fortitude – Courage

Living my own life has not been easy. For most of my formative years, I lived life based on the advice and expectations of others. Once I became conscious and began to believe in myself and became self-aware, I saw life differently. This took me into conflict with my old paradigms and with the people I had brought with me into those paradigms. When I broke the old patterns, I ran into conflict with those near me who felt it was their responsibility to give me unwanted advice. It took courage to make a hundred and eighty degree turn and begin to live the life that I intuitively knew I truly want to live.

Living Life My Way

I shall dare to live today,
I shall put aside my sorrows
    And disappointments,
I shall embrace the chance to live life my way.

I shall dare to be me.
I shall persist in believing
I am worthy of my own dreams;
I shall persist in making them all come true.

I shall ignore my doubts,
And the naysayers
Who say it is not possible,
That I do not have what it takes
        To make it happen.

Every time I fall,
I shall bounce right back up.
I shall shake the dust from my feet,
The disappointment from my mind,
And continue to walk forward
In spite of my fatigue from trying
Over and over again
        Without any sign
That I will be able to make it to the end.

I shall keep the goal line in sight,
And persist one step at a time,
Until I hear the crowds cheer,
And feel the joy of being me.
I shall be who I want to be,
And do what I want to do.
I shall wallow like a pig in the mud
In the satisfaction of living life my way.

Week 9, Day 2
Fortitude – Persistence

Persistence is pushing through to the point of self-actualization, nothing more and nothing less, to where and when I know I have finally arrived at my destination. This is not about being narcissistic. It is not even about being selfish. It is about believing in myself, and my thoughts, hopes, and dreams, and persisting until they all come true.

Knowing What Matters

What matters now to me
    Is me, just "me".
The years have taken away
    The "other" in me,
Leaving me,
    Just me,
    Alone with me.

My old dreams
Have vanished like shadows
Under the light of the truth that is me,
No ego, no hopes to be someone
I do not want to be,
No desire to do something
I do not want to do.

Old dreams,
Too heavy to carry,
Have been laid to rest
In the shell of the old me,
That has been laid to rest
In the graveyard
Of my dying thoughts.

And here I am!
        Come!
Celebrate me with me.
Celebrate the child that has become a man,
Who knows which path to take,
Having walked down all the other paths
That have led to nowhere.

Like the rat in the maze,
I having been manipulated by the unseen hand,
But I have found the source of the sacred pellet;
I have tasted the secrets of joy and love;
I have dined on the fruits of my own spirit;
I have been at the feast of my own soul.

Week 9, Day 3
Fortitude – Staying Focused

The key to fortitude is staying true to my dreams in spite of negative circumstances and negative feedback from others. Above all, I must stay the course in spite of my own negative thoughts bouncing around in those neural circuits of my brain. My mind is not capable of manifesting whatever it wishes because it can only use the physical energy that is available. But my Higher Self has the energies of the universe to accomplish whatever it wishes as long as I stay centered in peace and purpose and as long as my purpose is aligned with the greater good. I have to believe in myself and my greater mission. I must stay grounded in those beliefs, and I must be determined to stay the course until I can feel centered and in charge of my perceived realty. Above all, I must stay centered in just *being* and let the *doing* take care of itself through the powers of the universe.

What Matters

What matters now is just today,
This moment of moments where I am free
To just float with the notes of my favorite song,
Take flight on the cool ocean breeze,
Sail to the four corners of my world,
Soar higher, ever higher, ever higher,
Until I touch the alpha and the omega.
And be one with all that is and will be,
One with those whom I love,
And those who love me;
                    Forever young,
                    Forever beautiful,
                        Forever me.

Week 9, Day 4
Fortitude – Resilience

Fortitude includes my ability to bend in difficult situations. It is knowing when to charge full steam ahead and when to slow down or alter my course for the long term gain. I have to walk forward but at the same time keep my eyes and mind open to the new and different circumstances that the universe may bring onto my path.

I Can Bend

The old tree outside my door
Bends with the north east winds,
Refuses to snap and break,
Endures the dry hot summer months
And sheds its leaves in August.
It conserves its strength,
Hangs on to the life giving moisture,
Builds the resolve it will need
To endure another winter,
And patiently waits for another spring.

And I too am resilient.
I endure the cold touches of people
Whom I love,
Who are supposed to love me.
I refuse to snap; I refuse to break.
I too pull back my resources;
I place them beyond the reach of my heart
That wants to give all for one more kiss.
I steel my mind to one purpose,
And prepare to move on yet again.
I will shed no more tears.
I will desperately hold on
To those precious drops of moisture

That will be needed when I choose to try again.

Week 9, Day 5
Fortitude - Strength of Mind

My mind is designed to manage my life by seeking pleasure and avoiding sources of pain. That is a good thing. Granted it has to be directed by my Higher Self, but it still has important biological and psychological functions. My administration center, my mind, has to make thousands of decisions a day for me to survive and thrive. As such, it has to be nurtured and supported. I have to exercise, eat the right foods, and provide periods of restoration though good sleep habits and daily meditation. My healthy mind is a strong mind.

My Strong Mind

When the dawn breaks too early,
And sleep is so hard to find,
When I toss and turn throughout the night,
Dreading the work I do that rips my brain to shreds,
When I hate the mundane nature of my life
That puts my mind into perpetual neutral,
I make a conscious decision to rise again.
I put on my shoes and dress for the day,
To do what I have to do.

Though my mind tries to tell me it is weak,
I convince it that it must be strong.

When my tired mind waffles and wains,
And the thought of being me
Scrambles the neurons of my brain,
And the past laughs at my attempts to figure it out,
And my future cowers behind the blackened walls of doubt,
I seek the sanctuary of my physical and spiritual home.
I search out a place to sleep and escape from the day.
I ignore the sequence of messages crisscrossing my mind.
I fake it until I make it;
I find my way.
I pretend; I smile;
I am me; I am strong;
I am the person I want to be.

Week 9, Day 6
Fortitude – Being Stout-Heartedness

Fortitude is more than just pursuing my hopes and dreams; it is staying true to those things that really matter to my heart. It is important to remember that my main purpose is to expand and grow, and that my growth comes from my expanded abilities to absorb and give back the energies of love.

The most important things, those things that really matter, are my relationships. It is keeping my important relationships in focus at all times. If I gain the whole world and in the process lose my connections with those I love, I will have sacrificed the primary for the secondary, the core of myself for the external accomplishments of my mind.

If I stay centered in my heart, and if I keep the love energy flowing, I will inevitably have the physical and emotional power to realize all my hopes and dreams. Having a strong heart includes love for myself, love for my intimate ones, and love for my fellow conscious and unconscious human beings. It is through these combined love connections that I have the power to make a difference in my own corner of the world.

Wanting What I Really Want

My wants?
I have none, except to touch minds,
To share what I have learned,
The ability to avoid the pitfalls
Of disillusionment and depression,
To recognize those signs that take me down,
To escape the harshness of the dangerous places
Where minds are twisted and hearts are broken,
To avoid the road that should not be walked alone.

My wants?
I have none except to leave something behind,
Perhaps create a safe path,
Where my children and grandchildren can stroll
Free of the cares of this world,
Free to be who they are,
And live a life they will truly love to live.

My wants?
I have none,
Except to add my voice
To the chorus of voices that have learned
What it means to be alive among the dead,
To sing a perfect hallelujah
Among the cacophony of chaos,

To draw patterns in the sand
That the sea of life cannot wash away
With the next tide.

My wants?
I have none,
Except to be a peace with my fellow man,
To be at peace with the world of dreams,
To be at peace with my aging body,
To be at peace with the desires of my heart,
To be at peace with my neglected soul,
And to be at peace with my struggle for peace.

Week 9, Day 7
Fortitude – Strength of Soul

If my mind and heart are strong, then my soul is free to pursue those things that are eternal. If my body and mind are in balance with the desires of my heart, I can remove all the impediments to spiritual living. I can operate on the energies of love which are the food of my soul. My Higher Self can then operate with full authority connecting to the source and to the combined power of conscious human beings. We can expand and grow into the powerful beings we were meant to be.

Courage on Getting Older

One more spring, one more summer,
The years are counting down;
Soon I will leave this world
In the chariot of fire that I have found.

I see the path of death ravage through my family.
My brothers and sisters have left this place;
The moments of togetherness now are gone;
I face these years without their warm embrace.

One more fall, one more winter,
Still time to make a new memory,
Still time to rest before the warm fire,
And watch the days pass into eternity.

No regrets, no sorrows,
No call for courage to face the night,
No burden to lay down,
Just this moment to keep in sight.

One more fall, one more winter,
The years are counting down;
Soon I leave this world
In the chariot of fire that I have found.

Week 10
Gentleness

Gentleness is the virtue of doing good with the least possible harm to others. It is the decision to approach others from a stance of love rather than indifference. If we are gentle, we will offer a deep appreciation for each other's situation and point of view, and we will respect and preserve the dignity of everyone we meet. Gentleness is the outward demonstration of a heart-centered life.

Week 10, Day 1
Gentleness and the Spiritual

Gentleness is living in the sacred moment. It begins when I welcome the day in a state of worship. I take off my shoes because I walk on holy ground. I begin to sense the universal presence of the spirit of life and love that surrounds me each and every moment that I live. I just have to stop and open the eyes of my soul and embrace this sacred moment with the arms of my gentle spirit.

This Sacred Moment

The sacred morning begins with a sensuous caress;
The dark sky lifts its veils of soft blues and violets;
The choir of song birds break the hush with melodious tones,
And the air smiles as it kisses my soul with a gentle kiss.

And a new day begins, filled with blessings so profound
That my finite mind cannot comprehend them.
So it passes the honor on to my waiting heart
That joyously fills with love for self and love for life.

My love expands and grows to enfold those closest to my heart,

Until it overflows with love for all those I have ever known;
I understand the profound sacredness and embrace the ALL,
As my hands reach out to touch everyone with a gentle touch.

So soft is my world;
So fresh is the scent of the ocean;
So mellow is the touch of the forest;
So tender are these sensations that enfold me;
So soothing is the essence that embraces my soul;
So gentle is the sweet spirit that silently binds me to itself.

Week 10, Day 2
My Gentle Soul

When I greet each day with my gentle spirit, I begin to understand the nature and wholeness of my connection with Mother Earth. Through my masculine soul's interaction with the sacred feminine, I become a conscious person who walks gently on the Earth and touches my fellow man with a gentle touch.

Covenant with the Sacred Feminine

The sacred feminine is the matrix of creation.
She is the divine light to my soul.
She has been birthed in my body
By the gift of life from my mother,
Who gave me her own blood,
Her own body, her own female soul.
She shared her primal mystery with me,
So that through her, I too can understand,
And share in the mystery of the creation of life.

Therefore, I sacrifice my divine masculine
On the altar of the sacred feminine.
Through the power of my submission,
I combine her gentle spirit with my innate drive
To love, guide, and protect her.

Through this covenant,
I learn to cherish life itself,
And so I become the protector
Of all living things.

When I deny my divine connection
To the mystery of the feminine,
And plow blindly ahead
With my misguided masculine mind,
I deny my connection to the earth,
And I cut my world off from the only source
That can heal, nourish, and transform her.

When I deny her ageless wisdom
That carries the ancient memories,
I detach my soul from the source
That gives meaning to my life,
Which nourishes my mind with what is real.

I need to honor her presence
Within this masculine body,
And within my masculine soul;
I need to cherish the ground I walk on,
And the air I breathe,
I need to kiss the Earth softly,
And touch her body with a gentle touch.

Week 10, Day 3
My Gentle Heart

When I get in touch with my gentle spirit, I begin to experience the presence and activity of my loving gentle heart. I realize that it is not just a physical organ that pumps blood, but it is also the core of my spiritual body, the fourth and centering chakra.

The universe in its infinite wisdom has given me my life-mate so that I may truly understand the meaning of heart love. It is a love that has grown from passion into intimacy and into wanting the best for each other. My heart has the ability to share this love with other conscious souls. It spreads this love to everyone it touches, and it always touches with a gentle touch.

Heart Love

My heart cries out to you, my love,
To touch you gently with its hands,
To feel every part of your body that it loves.
 Its love vibrations flow into you,
And softly, tenderly enfold you.
My heart's voice pleads passionately,
To become one with you.

Love unites us with each other,
And with the giver of life,
And the author of love.
We become one in heart.
As our bodies begin to blend,
A divine chemistry is created
By the all-knowing,
To bind us to each other in body,
So that through our union,
Others may be conceived and born.

We become one in mind.
We set goals,
Combining each other's hopes and dreams,
To form one mind, one purpose,
So that the ones we bear can be raised
With the unity of two minds with one mind.

We become one in spirit.
Our souls begin to resonate with one vibration,
Growing with the love we give each other,
An ever expanding burst of divine love energy
That enfolds the children we bear,
Forming a cocoon of love for them,
A safe place for them to grow
Into the people they will be,
So that they too can emerge into the world
Of spirit-filled people,
Who give to each other the gentle touch of love.

Week 10, Day 4
Creating a Gentle Mind

When my heart and soul are joined through love, they begin to influence my mind. When I come to a heart and soul understanding of life, I begin to realize the nature of my physical brain, the creator and administrator of my thoughts. Left to its own devises, my mind will be focussed on self-preservation, the competition for status and recognition, and the accumulation of resources. Under its control, I can be insensitive to the needs of others; I can be harsh and cruel. However, once under the influence of my heart and soul, I become other-centered, longing to touch others with love energy from my heart and wisdom from my soul. I learn to think gentle thoughts.

Gentle Thoughts

Because I believe,
I zealously guard my thoughts,
Setting aside feelings of hopelessness and helplessness,
Ignoring my emotions of fear, shame, and anger.
I quiet my mind and embrace the center of my soul.

Soon the miracle begins.
As my soul touches my brain,
My essence begins to flow in concentric patterns,
And the rhythm of my soul soothes my mind.

With each gentle breath,
The feelings and emotions transform,
Shifting their energies from hopelessness to hope,
From hope to belief, from belief to power,
From power to gentle touches that change my world.

I begin to breathe in slow deep breaths.
Peace and love flood my whole being
As the creative fertility of my soul makes love to my mind.
They begin to breathe and sway in harmony with each other,
Giving birth to thoughts filled with love for all who seek peace.

Week 10, Day 5
Gentle Words

Thoughts are composed of images and feelings. When I put thoughts into words, my brain forms clear and defined concepts which link up to other concepts to create mind sets. When I employ these mind sets, think these thoughts, and speak these words, they become empowered, and as such, can be used to hurt or to heal. If they are just a product of my mind, they will be aimed towards powerful self-centered forces that are designed to protect and project the self. When they are channeled through my heart, they become instruments of love and healing.

Let my Words be Gentle

Words projected from images of fear
    From a weary mind,
Spoken in well-chosen phrases,
While its friends the eyes
Search the faces for signs
    Of acceptance or rejection,
Cautiously, fearfully,
Treading through the tangled pathways
Of other people's minds.

Words connected through feelings and sensations
    To my ever-beating heart,

Sensing, creating,
And sending out touches of kindness,
        Instruments of healing,
Channels of love and hope to other searching eyes.
Let my words be the children of thoughts from my soul,
That sees the world through loving eyes,
Always searching the faces of others for pieces of love,
Moments of togetherness.

Oh please, spirit that inhabits my heart,
        Please speak for me.
Let my words be kind and sensitive,
Honoring the fragile nature of the ones I touch,
Who seek only to be seen and heard.
        Let me pause and quietly listen
To the desperate words of those in need.

Le my ears be willing to listen,
To the sacred offerings of others.
Let my words be the product of my heart
        And not just my mind,
Free of the need to be respected and worshipped,
Reborn in the heart's desire,
To feel, to care, and to love.
Let my words be well-chosen, bending my thoughts,
So my thoughts can bend to the needs of others,
        So that we can grow together,
Sharing our essence in a dark and dreary world.

Week 10, Day 6
Gentle Actions-The Divine Masculine

When I unite my high priest with my high priestess, I combine power with gentleness. I become the Divine Masculine having the spiritual gift to be strong of mind, heart, and spirit, but gentle in my thoughts and actions. I can still reach for my dreams; I can still overcome all obstacles blocking my way to self-actualization; I can still be a warrior who fights for the truth; but I will fight not just for myself, but for the people I love. I become the protector, the guardian of the voiceless. I can reach the highest levels of ascension, but more importantly, I can stay here in my community, grounded and centered, and ready to lend a helping hand to those in need.

My Divine Masculine

Today, after many days,
I have become the man I want to be.
I have the power to use my mind
To determine what has to be done,
And to use the power of my body
      To make it so.

I have the wisdom to see the needs of those I love,
And the will to do what has to be done
To guide and protect them to the infinite good.
But I am gentle, only giving assistance when it is asked for,
Understanding that assistance not asked for is criticism.

And I have the power to set aside
My own wants and needs,
And to help a brother get back on the path,
Carrying his burden until he is strong enough
To carry it himself.
And I have the ability to do what I need to do
To set aside the power of the masculine,
To embrace the gentleness of the feminine,
To see inward but to act outward,
To do what must be done
For the good of those I love,
And for those I chance to meet upon the path,
So that together we can become the divine.

Week 10, Day 7
Staying Centered and Grounded

This is the final day in our ten weeks inspirational journey. I have explored what it means to be grounded. I believe in myself. I am aware of myself as a beautiful and powerful being. I accept myself unconditionally: who I have been in the past, who I am in the now, and whom I will become in the future. I recognize I have the ability to hear two voices and the power to choose the voice of my Higher Self, which will always guide me to the right decision for the greater good. And I forgive myself for all the wrongs I have done and all the wrongs that have been done to me so that I can live in power and freedom in the present.

Once thoroughly grounded in these truth, I have moved on to centering myself in my physical and spiritual life. I have rid myself of all my negative energy and focus on creating and emitting only the positive. I am grateful for all the contributions which conscious and unconscious people have made to my life. I appreciate life and all its gifts. I am content within the deepest regions of my soul, having centered the past with the future by living in the present. I am fortified by my beliefs and my knowledge of who I am and what I can accomplish. I have set a new course in life, and have the courage to go and do it. And finally, I have become a gentle human being. I am kind to myself and to others. I live an enchanted life.

I Am the Center of my Universe

I am thankful for all that has been,
All the pleasure and pain
That have made me who I am.
I am thankful for all the people
Who have guided me to this place
At the center of my universe,
The conscious who have nudged me
In the right direction,
And the unconscious who have shown me
The path I must not take.

And I am content being who I am.
I am at peace with what I have done.
I see the future as a lush garden,
Where I can bloom and produce
The fruits of my thoughts and words.

I have arrived in this place of being
Where I see the full dimension of life,
And appreciate who I have become.
        I am me,
    The ME I was meant to be.

I see the world in all its glory
In spite of the efforts of my fellow man
To destroy all that is by nature beautiful.

And I am strong.
I can move mountains with my heart and mind.
I can see a path through the wilderness,
And have the courage to walk it.
Regardless of what others say
I can and cannot do,
I have the wisdom to see what can be,
And the power to make it so.

And above all I am gentle,
With myself and with my fellow man.
I see that we are all on a difficult journey
To self-actualization,
Where we all may choose
The path of destruction from our mind,
Or the path that is good from our soul.
I recognize that others
May be conscious or unconscious
Of who they are and what they are doing,
            But I am gentle,
Tenderly nudging my fellow man
In the direction of the path
Where they can see who they are
And whom they can become.

Above all I am gentle with myself,
Recognizing that in this present life
I have the right to choose a path
That I think will lead to glory,

But I know that it is okay to wander from time to time
Away from that path,
Knowing and trusting that my heart and mind
Will usher me back to my journey's end,
Where I will become the man I want to be.

I am grounded;
I am centered;
I live an enchanted life.

Made in the USA
San Bernardino,
CA